Back to Utopia

"Life's First Gift"

Braun Media, LLC
11763 95th Avenue North
Maple Grove, MN 55369
763-416-9028
www.bmsdigital.com

Publisher
Tim Braun

Typographer
Christopher R. Mihm

Associate Publisher
Jean Paulsen

Cover Photographer
Jordi Gomez

Managing Editor
Dana Demas

Cover Art and Design
Julia A. Wolf

www.terrylyles.com

Back to Utopia

"Life's First Gift"

Terry Lyles, Ph.D.

Table of Contents

Table of Contents

Acknowledgments

I want to thank everyone who worked on this book with me to reach the people who will experience more of my life and passion to help others. Special thanks to Dana Demas for assisting me in this work. Her stellar commitment and creativity have influenced the final efforts that are reflected in the contents. Thanks to my boys, Brandon and Brent, for the many stories and life references that have shaped my life and beliefs forever, and for always understanding the impact that our lives have on all who read or receive this message. Thanks to Migdalia Cruz for working tirelessly with me to coordinate and control my schedule, and for always being available to assist with my family while I am away from home. To my mom Dale and my sisters Becky and Mary for life experiences from youth until today. To Janet Sweitzer for her creative ideas and input that have shaped this work and, ultimately, my life today. To my business associate, Chris Galli, for his commitment to help me move into the future with financial awareness. And finally, thanks to Tim Braun and his team at Braun Media for believing in me and enabling my message of hope and courage to reach the masses.

Introduction

It's not what happens to us in life that defines us, it is our *response* to what happens.

So many of us are searching for a better life. We think the answers to more happiness, more love or more success lie outside of us. We lament that we don't have the job we want or a better relationship or simply enough time in the day to enjoy our lives, and we wait for someone or something else to save us. In reality, we have the answers. We hold the key to our wildest dreams by changing our perception.

Life is full of stress and it's not going away anytime soon! In fact, it *shouldn't* go away because we as people are forged in these moments of crisis, failure and disappointment.

The challenges and stresses of life are *gifts* waiting to be unwrapped.

How you manage stress will determine whether you simply *survive* life or whether you *thrive* in life. Stress itself is not the problem. Your response in the face of that stress is what matters—and it also happens to be the only thing you can control.

Receiving *the gift* is as simple as rising to the occasion, each and every day, no matter what life throws your way. Life isn't fair. When you learn to accept the facts and limitations of your life, you begin to transform that life into something greater. There is no shortcut. We must go *through* our tough times to emerge from them and find the life that's waiting for us. We are the architects of our journey.

The Gift is designed to help guide you through this process of reaching your full potential. Your best self is in there! It's merely waiting to be cultivated. This book is based on what I've learned from years of helping people achieve better lives, whether they're professional athletes seeking to maximize their performance or couples in marriage counseling hoping for a better relationship. Ultimately, the principles are the same.

Each Chapter takes you through a dimension of life that puts all of us to the test at one time or another. Mastering these dimensions by changing your perception will yield the key to changing your life.

I hope you enjoy this book as much I've enjoyed writing it. Ultimately, how we respond in the face of life's challenges is *The Gift*, to ourselves, to others and to the world. Ready to get started?

Chapter 1
Back to Utopia

"The world breaks everyone and afterward, some are strong at the broken places."
– Ernest Hemingway

Infants are all born the same. When you look at a baby, you understand that a baby needs regular rest, regular food and a similar type of care. Babies may differ in their temperament, but what they need is the same at a basic level. You never meet an infant who wants a steak dinner or a beer to take off the pressure!

It sounds funny, but this truth belies a deeper truth: adults are also wired to need the same things. All adults—men and women—have similar needs on a physiological level because we're all born the same. An infant cries when he or she is hungry, tired or physically uncomfortable. As adults, we suppress these "cries" and stop listening to our bodies. We don't train our bodies to meet these similar basic needs and we suffer the consequences, physically, mentally, emotionally and spiritually.

In other words, we are wired to survive and especially thrive, but our programming gets in the way.

We are all products of our conditioning. It's important to recognize the bad programming we've become accustomed to and not go on automatic pilot simply because that's the way we've been (mistakenly) taught to live. How many of us eat two or three times a day? Or skimp on proper rest and relaxation because we simply have too much to do? The problem with this "program," which is the one most Americans live their lives by, is that *it works against our basic needs*.

As women and men, we respond to bad programming after we're born, despite having these needs or wiring. We only eat 2-3 times a day, when we need to eat 5-6 times a day. We may need less sleep than infants, but we neglect the rest we need, which doesn't change. As adults, rest is how we grow mentally, spiritually, emotionally and physically in energy, though we don't grow in our bodies. Rest is spiritual and sleep is physical (more on this later).

I always say my kids are older than me now—my son Brent is 20 and my son Brandon is 22. What I mean is that kids grow past you eventually, but then they come back around and realize they don't know as much as they think they do.

There can be a similar journey for all adults. How infants function should be the template for adults, too, in more ways than not. We can go back to the beginning, when we were wiser. Adults have stopped doing what they're wired to do and that's when functioning drops.

Health, happiness and productivity all stand to benefit when we realize this simple truth.

WHERE'S MY UTOPIA?

When we're born as infants, we've left a utopian state. A mother's womb is the perfect environment. We're never tired, never hungry, never thirsty. We have no relationship issues. We're alone, totally connected to what we need and the most important thing. A developing baby must think, "*Hey, I own this thing! I'm totally controlled, happy and taken care of…and I've never known any different.*"

Then we're born! We're cold, slimy and spitting mucus out of our lungs and we think, "*What happened? My automatic 'drive-through' umbilical cord is detached!*" The moment we're born is the first experience of crisis in our lives.

As a result, we're wired for crisis. We're born into the most volatile state you can imagine. Birth for human beings is like throwing someone off a cliff and saying swim! The body interprets this exit from the womb as tragedy and as death, until it realizes it can handle this new and changing environment. The baby can learn to breathe, get warm again and find nourishment. Food, comfort and oxygen now come from the environment, not the mother's womb.

However, we will spend the rest of our lives looking for that utopian experience in the womb. We search for it in achievement, in love and in virtually every other way. We seek comfort and perfection.

Think about how many times you've said, "*If only I had this, my life would be perfect.*" The object is different for everyone, and some of us have more than one object at different moments in time that we believe will lead us to the perfect life.

We want perfect love. We want to be monogamous and be the most important person in another person's life. The Greek word "genes" (genesko) is the root of the word "know." Genesko means to ingest or impregnate. So to know and be known is akin to being inside of somebody. When we idealize that perfect partner—whether having high expectations of our current partner or longing for the perfect partner we don't currently have, we are desiring to be known completely. We almost want to be inside of this person. It's the difference between knowing of someone and actually knowing someone. You feel it from inside you.

We want perfect health. We think, "*If I could just afford a personal trainer,*" or "*If I just had more time to workout.*" or "*If I just didn't have this health problem, everything would be...perfect.*"

We also want perfect stability, whether financially, in our careers, as a person or in our relationships. We don't want things to change. We want to hold onto the moment instead of spending it freely, even when the moment isn't so great. But change is inevitable, even in the perfect environment we started out in. (After all, we were all born weren't we?)

In fact, the tragedy and pain of change is what creates life. If we stayed in the womb indefinitely, we never would have been born. We never would have loved. We never would have achieved. We never would have lived our lives and discovered our potential as a person in the world with all of its stresses and imperfections. Stress is the gift, but only if you appreciate what it can do *for* you, not what it does *to* you.

STRESS "UTILIZATION"

People are obsessed with living longer and looking younger. Just look around at all of the anti-aging products and information out there. Every day there is a new get-young gimmick that people think is going to be the magic key to more success, more happiness or more self-esteem. All of these surgeries and cosmetic procedures promise to fight off the progression of time and the toll life takes on our bodies. We're literally trying to fight gravity.

Gravity keeps us on the earth, both in a physical sense and in a larger, metaphysical sense. Gravity also may be anything that has the potential to bring stress or negative events to us. We first learn about gravity when we are young. We may try to jump off a ledge or the bed and we fall, hurting ourselves. A child may think the thrill of the fall was fun, but hitting the ground was not. Hopefully the child does not hurt him or herself badly, but still learns an important lesson: when you jump, you are going to fall and eventually land. Falling can be exciting, but landing is the challenge. That's gravity. We may not understand it by name at the time, but it's a lesson that must be learned, over and over again throughout our lives.

As adults, gravity expands in its meaning. Gravity becomes anything that may cause us stress as we navigate our daily lives. It could be rush hour traffic, floods from too much rain, a difficult family member, bills or your ex.

Normally we say, "*Oh, if I could just get rid of these things, everything would be ok.*" People try to avoid stress in the hope that their life will come closer to the state of balance and happiness they seek. But it won't! Stress is not only unavoidable, it's also what makes us who we are because it forces us to respond and build strength in response to it. We become who we are because of the stresses in our lives if we use them correctly.

Whatever we can't change in our lives is gravity. For me, it's having a special needs child. My son, Brandon, has been a quadriplegic since the age of one, and twenty-one years later we still don't know why. It's a fact of my life that is never going to change. The way I respond to it and learn from it is what has made the difference in my life and continues to make me a better person every day. Brandon has been one of my *greatest gifts* in helping me to become a better man and do the work that I do.

Just like the child jumping off the ledge, as adults we need gravity to continue teaching us about life and our potential strength in the face of it.

GRAVITY'S GIFT

I have a client who was recently diagnosed with cancer. The cancer is Stage III, possibly Stage IV, and she may not have more than a year to live. Her tumor is the size of a baseball. She's devastated because her life as she knows it is over. It's a tragedy, no question; however, I've tried to tell her there's something positive that can come out of it. If she takes her disease as an opportunity to live her life to the fullest in the time she has left, she's allowing the diagnosis to affect her in the most positive way possible. It's a change in awareness.

That's gravity—you can't totally stop disease. You can fight it, but you can't stop it. All you can control is the way you respond to it. Sometimes it takes the urgency of a terminal illness to bring us to this realization. Remember before, when I talked about stress as the greatest opportunity for change and growth? It's true, but it doesn't have to be life-threatening stress if you can change your perception sooner: you've got to create your world, every step of the way, *no matter what*, because life is not perfect. It's not utopia here! This is the world, and the beauty is that it's out there for the choosing. The bad news is that you can screw it up. That delicate equilibrium is the difference between a good life and a bad life, and the power is in your hands.

Living life with the awareness that you're never going to find perfection, but rather that you have to create it, is "The Gift." The English word "perfect" comes from an old Greek word that literally means "complete." To seek completion instead of perfection is the gift!

Everybody has the gift—it's in our DNA, but most people don't unwrap it. We're carrying around this Christmas gift for years and we don't open it. What's in it could be the key to your happiness and your wildest dreams, both of which *you* create.

So why don't most people take advantage of the power that's inside of them? Past failures or bad experiences with our parents can make us scared to open this gift, because our expectations haven't been met in the past. We've looked for utopia over and over again, but feel so let down when we don't find it that we stop trying. We stop believing. But it's still inside of us.

The bottom line is that life stinks many days. You've got to make it something. Common people become *great* people because they navigate life differently than others. What many fail to realize is that tragedy and disaster are the greatest vortex for learning. Stress is the real mechanism to cause people to make real change. People just don't like change. We're creatures of habit—that's our wiring.

My son's handicap is a gift. It ultimately ruined my marriage. I felt angry. I felt guilty. I finally decided that I could either wallow in it and allow it to destroy every aspect of my life, or I could kick it and turn it into something positive. For everything that's right with me, there's something equally wrong that I've converted. What makes me good makes me bad, and the same is true for every person on this planet.

I'm attracted to crisis because I've had crisis in my life and it's the most potent source of change. When I flew halfway around the world to work with tsunami victims in Thailand, I was forever changed by the strength of the people I encountered there. These were people who'd lost everything—loved ones, their homes, all of their possessions—but they managed to go on. We've already forgotten about the tsunami, a cataclysmic event that saw 250,000 people killed in 90 minutes and devastated the lives of millions of others. However, it was a life-defining event for millions of people who could find life-meaning in the midst of tragedy. Once again, the gift must be unwrapped to discover and appreciate it.

FROM HERE TO UTOPIA

I teach people how to become more aerodynamic and deal with these "gravities" in their lives so they're sources of strength and transformation rather than negative drains. Today we have so much more gravity pulling us away from our balance in a negative way. We have so many pressures to own the right house or car, wear the right clothes, or engage in all of the modern diversions from email to video games, which are designed to make our lives easier or more enjoyable, but end up doing the exact opposite.

All the while we're looking for that utopian perfection in relationships, in health, in love and in life, but all of these things in our world can pull us the other way. Bad foods, bad people and diversions that feel good in the moment, but are ultimately bad for you in the long run, pull you even farther from that balance into a free fall with a rough landing.

Every one of us will spend our lives looking for that utopian state we lost so long ago. Will we ever find it? Probably not. But by learning how to avoid the distractions and effectively respond to what is (the gravities, particular to your life!), you can make the journey a whole lot more enjoyable *and* productive.

Chapter 2
Time *Is* On Your Side

"Put your hand on a hot stove for a minute, and it seems like an hour. Sit with a pretty girl for an hour, and it seems like a minute. That's relativity."
– Albert Einstein

Time is our greatest currency. You can't invest it. You can't save it. The only thing you can do is spend it. The greatest gift you can give someone is your time. Throughout my career and in my personal life, I've sat and talked with many people as they are dying. They always tell me that the gift they treasure most is time spent with loved ones.

Children also teach us that time is very precious. What do kids want when they are young more than your time? (And maybe the newest video!) When I had my boys, I would intentionally spend time with them every day. I would make sure I spent at least a half-hour a day just with them—wrestling and knocking me down, just sitting around talking, asking me questions, or whatever they wanted to do. I gave them total access, with no distractions or multi-tasking, and I put all of my energy and thoughts into them. It was an investment that I knew, someday, would help make them into great adults. And today they both make me very proud.

Like a deferred IRA, this time investment can't be spent immediately. We don't actually invest in time, but rather spend that time with people or learning that can become the investment payoff. Your children don't know it and you may not even know it when you're in the thick of raising them, but what you're giving them is a gift. Eventually, a child turns into a person and realizes this investment helped make them who they are (usually after adolescence, when they don't appreciate it!). For children, time expenditure creates an investment portfolio that can be cashed in later in life.

For adults, time is a currency designed to be spent now.

This became resoundingly clear when my son Brandon was diagnosed as an infant with a terminal illness and it rocked my world. At the time, I thought I had my life figured out. I had it all planned! I was married, had a child and a budding career and suddenly all of those plans didn't mean anything because this tragedy had interjected itself into my plans.

I would spend all night awake sometimes, watching my son and hoping he would stay alive. Brandon was diagnosed after he began having seizures and muscle spasms and weight loss at ten months old. For many years, we didn't know if Brandon would live through another year. We were always on edge. We were told he'd only survive until five years old, then 10, always with constant testing. We still have no diagnosis 22 years later—the medical term is "nowhere otherwise specified (NOS)."

I learned early on with my son, after days, weeks, months and thousands of hours of pain, emergency room visits and ambulance rides, that I finally had to learn to relax in that uncomfortable space. I came to the realization that I'm not going to let it beat me. Today, as troubling or as challenging as the moment is, it's all I've got. I'm going to extract all that I can from my situation.

I learned through this difficult situation that we eventually lose everything we care about through breakups, divorce and especially death. What really matters is how we spend the moments of time we have to live in *the now* every day. Yesterday is past, tomorrow is in the future, but today is the gift to be unwrapped and explored! The simple but profound choices we make every day become the branching off of a specific route of destiny that shows we have more influence than we realize. Every choice we make directs or even redirects the path of our lives with every person we meet and every circumstance we encounter, and this is all done through an awareness of the gift of time.

Ultimately, life is more important than our plan for it— in other words, responding to what life throws your way, rather than "achieving" life. I've had 20 years in training of appreciating time, no matter what. We tend to complicate time. Time is usually very simple.

WHAT IS TIME?

When we look at time, I define it as the vibrational distance between cause and effect, or the space between birth and death. Time is linear; you can't stop it. It's on a one-way journey from now to the end of time. We make a decision to spend time doing something every moment of our lives. For instance, right now you are reading this paragraph of this book instead of doing something else.

Sometimes, we decide to spend our time doing something that's not pleasant, like going to the dentist. We may have a difference in our attitude, but in essence, time is nothing more than a space and it's always the same. Our perception is what changes.

Albert Einstein's wonderful quote at the beginning of this chapter explains the concept of relativity. He once said: "Put your hand on a hot stove for a minute, and it seems like an hour. Sit with a pretty girl for an hour, and it seems like a minute. That's relativity."

Time is relative. Did time slow down with pain or speed up with pleasure? No. The interpretation of that space as pleasurable or painful determined how I perceived and spent my time in my space. We all have the ability to interpret that space known as time. Sometimes we go on autopilot and zone out. Sometimes we allow the events around us to determine how we feel. And sometimes, if we discover the gift, we decide how we are going to experience time.

Time is a mental focus: how you challenge your mind to draw a perception from that space makes all the difference. Time is moving whether you're in it or not, or whether you're happy or frustrated. You can't control time, but you can control your interpretation of it.

How we spend any space of time—no matter what's going on around us—is the gift. That's why you have to live in the present. Time is the gift of *now*, if you can look at it differently.

ALL CYLINDERS GO

One of the things you're taught in racecar driving is that when you're sliding towards the wall, don't look at it. If you look towards the wall when sliding in a racecar, your body will lock up accordingly, and you'll actually pull yourself to the wall. Look away, and your body makes millisecond adjustments, so you may not hit the wall as hard, or at all.

Our perception of time shapes our reality. People complain that their lives aren't what they want, but, in reality, they created it. Whatever you look for in life, you'll find—good or bad, healthy or unhealthy, exciting or boring. In time, what you look for is what you get.

We are naturally trained to focus on something we fear or a threat that seems dangerous. Our wiring primes us for it and it takes training not to do it. I teach people how to run on all cylinders in life, in every moment of time, for the best possible outcome. We all have four cylinders inside of us: the mental, emotional, spiritual and physical. Balance between the four is what drives us forward to our maximum capacity. Running with one or more of these elements out of whack is like trying to race a car with an 8-cylinder engine with only 2 spark plugs firing. You'd look under the hood and realize, *"No wonder it's not running!"*

An untrained mind is most dangerous because you end up getting exactly what you *don't* want. The biggest space in life is the one between your ears— *you have to control what you think and how you perceive time to make your life what you want it to be*.

When athletes learn this, they learn to control their perception of time. When I train an athlete in visualization, I tell them to think about what they want to achieve. A racecar driver literally envisions driving around the track, or a baseball player imagines going up to bat in the bottom of the ninth inning, with two outs and a man on third.

All well and good, but when you get on track at 200 mph and your heart is pounding and your competitors are racing by you, can you actually handle it? You can, because you've already been in control of your mind and this event before. I teach athletes how to literally slow time down during a high-pressure performance situation by visualizing the event in slow motion beforehand and learning to control it.

Everyone can benefit from the same visualization in their own life, even if they're not racing around a track at 200 mph. Visualizing what you want to achieve today or the person you want to meet today by spending the mental energy on it, creates the expectation that it will happen. Whatever you're looking for, visualize it and you will have a better chance of making it happen.

MEDITATION = CONTROL OF YOUR LIFE

Unfortunately, many people feel jaded or let down because of past bad relationships or professional failures. They're actually more focused on their regrets than on their dreams and desires and, as a result, get more of the former than the latter. You look for what you don't want by focusing on it.

18

Daily meditation offers a way out of that mindset and into a more positive one.

"Meditate," you say? *"I don't know how to meditate!"* That's the reaction I get from most people when I tell them to meditate on how they would like their lives to be. However, most people do know how to meditate; it's simply in the opposite direction. The average person spends one hour a day in negative thought, worrying. Do you know how to worry? How much time do you spend worrying about your kids, your bills or your relationship?

Worry is negative meditation. The word "worry" comes from a root word that means to "strangle" or "bite." In other words, *worry can get a stranglehold on you and keep you from living your life the way you're meant to.* The worry burns your mental, emotional, spiritual and physical energy *that could be better spent living.*

As a result, everyone is already an expert in meditation. You just need to change the focus!

Compelling research by psychologist Martin Seligman has found that people who recall three things they are grateful for each day experience significantly higher levels of happiness. One small change in perception produces a global change in outlook!

I tell people to spend some time every morning thinking about what they're grateful for, because we tend to be most imbalanced in the morning. Sleep regenerates us and gives us a clean slate to start over next day. The problem is that we usually wake up where we left off. We think about what's wrong or what we have to do, rather than the potential of a new day and all that we've accomplished before it. When we wake up and we're coming back to ourselves, we can think, *"I hate my life! My job is stressful,"* or *"I don't like who I'm sleeping next to."*

So you have to start the process as soon as you wake up. Lie there for two to five minutes and think of what you are grateful for to start the day out right.

URGENT VS IMPORTANT

Time is also about that lifelong search for utopia. Everyone is seeking how to maximize time. We want more time. We want to slow time down. We want to go back in time. How often do you catch yourself saying, *"If only I had more time, I could do this or that"*? The gift of time, just like stress, is all in how we learn to manage it.

Many times we get stuck doing "urgent" things. In corporate America, this is known as crisis management. But in business and in life, you have to stop and think, *"Did anybody die here? Is the world going to end"*? More often than not the answer is no, but we act as if life and death is on the line.

All this does is drain the productivity out of our day. We may feel like we are being productive or that we have no choice but to respond to these "crises," but in reality, our response is achieving the opposite. We are depleting ourselves from living and working as we should.

In these crisis moments, it's important to stop, pull back and analyze what's going on or what has taken place. Was it really that urgent? Or could you have responded differently? Could you have kept all four of those cylinders going—the mental, emotional, spiritual and physical—without getting out of balance with just one or two? For instance, an emotional explosion to a person or unexpected event takes you out of balance. So does physically pushing yourself to work beyond your natural limits by neglecting basic needs, like sleep and proper eating. If you can manage the urgency of the day in a way that's more focused on *balance* and *endurance*, you can invest in the importance of the day. If not, you end up doing a lot of urgent things, but not the important things.

This is where procrastination comes into play—basically an avoidance of time that sometimes results from all of these "urgent" things we have to do, which leaves us no time to do what we need to do. I have to make this call, so I avoid it and never do it. Or that stack of laundry has been sitting there taunting me for a week, but I don't do it and it keeps growing with each day.

Instead, why not make it a challenge and just do it? Sometimes, hesitation equals death. Military training teaches this. In the military, you need a response, which maximizes a space of time that could mean life or death. While most people's jobs and household chores are not a matter of life or death, it's still important to maximize your time for productivity and endurance. I know that I work best if I get the difficult things done early in the day, but every person is different and you have to find what works best for you.

HOW TO MAXIMIZE TIME

Time is also a space for learning, every day. You can either seize the moment and connect, or disconnect and let it pass you by. This goes for positive and negative experiences alike. It's all in the perception, as you're probably catching on by now.

There are those activities that everybody dreads. For instance exercise, which most people try to avoid or don't like. In reality, we need movement for our bodies, which also affects the other three cylinders: emotional, mental and spiritual health. All of our capacities can atrophy, simply without movement. The entire universe is in a state of movement and so are we. Vibration is a very slight movement, and it's always happening.

Movement is how we get in sync with a moment in time. Find a healthy distraction to make these unenjoyable things doable, instead of just checking out. When you hate working out, distract yourself by listening to music or reading a book. Music is great because it relaxes the mind and activates the creative right brain, putting you in sync with the moment or the person. If don't like going to church, sit next to someone you really like to make it go by faster and be more enjoyable. Remember Einstein's quote about relativity? You can't change time, but you can change how you experience it.

This goes for our relationships with people, too. As a parent, I learned more from my children than I ever taught them. My goal every day after my sons were born was to become their student. I wanted to really give them my focus and see them for who they are, as well as for what they have to teach me. I take this approach with relationships around me. When asked, I use this approach in my relationships to study the person in front of me. I say, *"I'm studying you—I want to know who you are today, because it's not the same ten years ago or yesterday."* I want to understand and admire the individual. All of this requires me to be fully present in those moments.

Sometimes, it scares people when you really look at them or want to know them. Living in the *now* is uncomfortable for many people because they're not happy with who they are or their lives, so they want a

23

distraction from themselves and also to distract others. I've spent my life extracting lessons from other people—learning from them by tuning into them. I can tell you that people are our greatest source of wisdom and pleasure.

Economist Juliet Schor, in her book, _The Overworked American_ (1993, Basic Books), estimates that the average person spends 163 more hours working today than in 1969, the equivalent of one month. The number of Americans holding down two or more jobs has nearly doubled in the same timeframe. All of this is in pursuit of the pot of gold at the end of the rainbow, when really, our pot of gold is right here for the taking in each other.

Most people don't get to the end of their lives and say, _"I wish I had spent more time working or studying the tax code or wearing more expensive clothes."_ What matters most is the people around them. If we can learn that early and live our lives accordingly, we stop spending more time with stuff and work than with people. Instead of looking through someone or living on automatic pilot in an endless cycle of urgency, it's about being present and absorbing another person. Make both communication and connection _intentional_.

The gift of time will create wonderful things or it will create nothing, depending on how we use it.

RETURN ON INVESTMENT

I talked earlier about all of the time I've spent dealing with my son Brandon's illness. It's been a gift that has not only allowed me to share in his pain and take some of that on for him, but it has also given me a sense of purpose and, when I least expected it, comfort.

My dad died suddenly a couple of years ago at 86 years old. He was sitting on the couch with my mom and suffered a heart attack, after having survived and recovered from three strokes. He was a strong man who had lived a great life, but I wasn't prepared for his death. When I got the phone call that he had passed away, it was from my sister Becky. She was hysterical and I could barely understand her. I immediately drove to my parents' house and got there about an hour later. My dad was lying on the floor next to the couch, where the paramedics had tried to revive him, unsuccessfully. In true crisis-management form, I took my mom and sister next door to the neighbors, and agreed to wait with my dad until the coroner arrived.

As fate would have it, the coroner got lost and took about 45 minutes to show up. That space of time was a challenge. I sat there next to my dad's body, overcome with emotion, but also trying to keep it together. However, in that unexpected time, I ended up telling him everything I would have wanted to say to him before he died. I cried and talked to him, and all the while, I felt that his presence was still in the room. I was so comforted sharing with him that I actually felt closure in talking to him there. I had shared that space of time with him.

During the eulogy at his funeral, I stood at the podium and saw my son Brandon sitting in the front row in his wheelchair. Brandon had always had a special connection to my dad, laughing and playing together throughout his life. As I choked up during the eulogy, I looked at Brandon. And though it's likely he wasn't registering any of what had happened to his grandpa, he comforted me in that moment. I looked at him and, in a simple glance, found that space of connection I had shared with him so many times before as he had a painful medical procedure done or a scary ride to the emergency room. It showed me the power of maximizing space and time, and the return benefit you always get.

Time is a commodity that must be optimized to experience the fullness of life. Therefore "The Gift" is time.

Chapter 3
Weakness Is Your Greatest Teacher

"Our strength grows out of our weaknesses."
– Ralph Waldo Emerson

Human weakness is the subject of great books, legendary movies and even the daily gossip around the water cooler because it's something we all struggle with. Weakness often explains why someone's life has taken a wrong turn or why we make poor decisions that we later regret. Why do we talk about the mistakes and weaknesses of others? Because our own weaknesses are often what we fear or struggle with the most in our lives. Think about how many times you hear the expression, "*I did it in a moment of weakness,*" to explain away an impulse buy or an eating binge or some other sort of temptation-gone-wrong.

However, the issue with weakness is that most people interpret it as something inferior, when, in reality, weakness is a gift if we allow it to teach us about ourselves. Weakness, more than anything, can deliver us to strength, but only if we submit to it.

Many of the greatest things on earth have been humbled to become what they are. Steel is heated and weakened to become finer. Gold is restructured to become a piece of jewelry. These metals are literally refined to make them into the building and ornamental materials we value so much. Gold is a precious metal, valued for its ability to withstand heat and stress. Rather than break, it remains intact by flowing through the experience. Likewise, as human beings, we are called to react to what life throws our way without breaking. We don't stop experiencing stress or weakness. We simply learn how to bend and continue growing, becoming something better because of it.

Ultimately, weakness is a transitional state between a state of imperfection and perfection. Once again, it's about flipping that coin. Is weakness going to drag you down or are you going to kick weakness and use it to achieve something greater? We can grow from a state of failure or struggle and turn that weakness into something great. Elite athletes and performers learn how to take the challenge that weakness presents and use it correctly, rather than as a threat. Supporting the alchemy of weakness into greatness doesn't mean you'll never experience weakness again or even that you'll get rid of the situation in which you feel weak. Rather, you change your mindset.

Weakness, more than anything, is an opportunity.

THE ALCHEMY OF GREATNESS

Weakness appears in many different guises, varying from one person to the next and even from one moment in our lives to another.

If each of us is made up of four elements—the mental, emotional, spiritual and physical—then weakness can occur in any of these capacities.

A mental weakness might be the inability to stay focused or to constantly fight with distraction. It could be a matter of brain chemistry, as in ADD or ADHD, but it also could be viewed as a strength. Most people who struggle with distraction are very creative people; they look at things in ways other people don't. I think of my son, Brent, this way. He's constantly looking around and finding and researching things that stimulate him. For someone who struggles with too much distraction, I would advise to oscillate better. Do anything for more than 90 minutes and you'll begin to flat-line, because we're designed to rest and recover our energy levels throughout our daily activities. All of us, but especially those who struggle with distractions, need frequent pit stops to keep running well and focus (more on this later).

For children, it's important to find the learning model that works for them. Our society trains children to learn the same way, but not everybody learns by sitting in a classroom, looking at the board and listening. Some kids need to touch and experience objects, and end up distracted because of this difference. Good teachers use different treatment modalities for different children, subtly, so they absorb the information as equals.

An example of an emotional weakness is someone who cares so much about people that they're constantly enabling them to stay in unhealthy or unproductive situations. These are the people who clean up other people's messes, whether their children, spouse, friends or other family members. They put up with irresponsible behavior or hurtful words and actions, and tend to make excuses for the other person. The problem is that if you're enabling people, you're actually hurting them, not helping them (not to mention hurting yourself and diverting the focus from what you want and need). People who help too much usually lack boundaries—they don't know what's too much. But if this tendency is converted into a strength, for instance, if you become a psychologist, you can help people in a healthy way. As long as you do it with the proper boundaries and self-awareness, it can be a great career.

A spiritual weakness plays on what we believe and how we believe it. An example would be an individual who only sees the best in everyone. Believing in people's goodness is a wonderful trait, and we may have too little of it in general. However, the reality is that not everybody intends to do their best, so the weakness becomes *"I'm always getting burned, because people take advantage of me or leave me hanging."* The strength could come from a different state of awareness that I'm not always going to get burned, because I've balanced my belief with an acceptance that not everyone is always going to act out of goodness. There are some people who are going to respond to me badly no matter what.

The most tangible example of weakness is a physical weakness. My son, Brandon, has been physically weak his entire life because he is confined to a wheelchair and can't do anything on his own. Most people would interpret that as total weakness, but he's one of the strongest people I know. His weakness has taught him to be tough. Even though he can't physically do anything, he's learned to use his charisma to get what he wants. He does it all the time and people don't even know it.

We were once in a mall walking around and there were three teenage girls. Brandon was looking at them and, before you know it, they walked up to him and said, *"Look how cute he is!"* Brandon looks small, maybe the size of a 7 or 8 year old, even though he's 22. Before long, these girls were kneeling down and touching his hand. And all the while, Brandon's looking at them smiling and thinking, *"You girls are beautiful and I still got your attention in a wheelchair!"* How many guys would love to do that? To have a group of three girls walk up to him and say, *"Hi, how are you?"* Other people may see Brandon's handicap as total weakness, but the way he has responded to it has changed that assumption.

Whatever kind of weakness and whatever the specifics to your individual life, a single truth remains: if you take those things that you cannot change and you convert them into inspiration, it will help you move through them quicker. *You* initiate the conversion process by deciding you will be challenged by weakness versus threatened by it.

Think of the caterpillar. It's a small, rather ugly insect that, when it thinks it's time to die, spins itself into a cocoon and, little does it know, comes forth later as a beautiful butterfly. The metamorphosis of caterpillar into butterfly could not have taken place if the caterpillar weren't up for the transformation, with no knowledge of what was to come after. The caterpillar prepares to die and emerges as the creature it's meant to be—more beautiful *and* more adapted to survive and thrive. So is a butterfly an improved caterpillar? Or is it its own thing? *It's a butterfly that came from the death of the old caterpillar self!*

Every religion believes there has to be a death to atone for life. *Weakness is the human classroom for our potential transformation into greatness.*

A LAZY MIND IS THE DEVIL'S WORKSHOP

My mom always used to say to me growing up, "*A lazy mind is the devil's workshop!*" And while she may have been referring to my laziness about chores, it can be broadened to include "a laziness" about helping ourselves throughout our lives. If we sit idle and wait for things to change, chances are, they're only going to get worse.

The paradox of the weakness-to-strength process is that we all feel weakness at times. The goal isn't to eliminate weakness, but rather, to not get stuck in it. The real question is: how long do you stay there? Weakness is always there to teach us a lesson, but there is a critical period for action. If we don't act, we might miss our opportunity and drift into apathy, anger, regret or self-pity. We might get stuck if we don't discover what weakness is there to teach us. Linearity is the problem, not the emotion itself. Weakness asks us to understand what it is, to allow it to educate us as much as possible, then to ask a better question. Instead of, "*Why me?,*" we should ask, "*How can I convert this to help me? How can I use this to get what I really want out of life?*" Otherwise, we flat-line—mentally, emotionally, spiritually and physically—and fail to learn weakness' lessons.

The need for action can be met, paradoxically, by surrendering ourselves to something or someone else. We must yield and lean into weakness by becoming servants in order for that to happen. The Bible says: "He that is great among you shall be your servant." Martin Luther King, Jr., echoed a similar sentiment in his *I Have A Dream* speech. He said the fight for equality wasn't about violence and aggression, but attitude. He knew the equal rights movement needed to be done in the right way, with passion. That's what made his speech so resounding at that point in history—he knew they were standing at a moment of potential greatness, but had to respond correctly.

By serving my son, Brandon, I've learned how to become strong. I've learned that it's not just about brute strength, but also about finesse. It's how I speak, my body language, my tone of voice and other skills that have been born out of my experiences with Brandon.

Many people might interpret being subservient to a person or a thing as weakness, but, in reality, the greatest way to help someone is to serve them. It's also the greatest way to help yourself.

SERVITUDE IS FORTITUDE

A good example of the power of servitude is in our intimate relationships. Women like men who are both weak and strong. Men who exhibit power under control, or in check, rather than overpowering her to get what he wants are much more successful in the long run. I always tell men: "*Quit trying to be an ape*! Try to serve her until she comes to you and, eventually, she'll tell you what she wants and needs, and you'll give it to her."

But you must inhabit a delayed gratification mindset to do it. You must submit to: *I'll serve you now, and get what we both want later.* Forcing the situation or making it about power gets you nowhere. A relationship is a living thing. Like a plant that grows from a seed with proper oxygen, water and light, you simply need to give your servitude enough time to germinate. A seed cannot produce its fruit unless it's first put into the ground and dies itself—once again, showing us the weakness required for becoming strong. When we truly serve each other, we find the love, acceptance and strength we seek.

Servitude can most powerfully transform our relationships with ourselves. Each year, 20 million people suffer from depression. Another 20 million suffer from anxiety disorders. We're the most depressed nation on the planet, yet we have the most opportunity for fulfilling lives.

One of the first prescriptions for someone who is depressed or anxious is to serve someone. Get out of yourself! Go volunteer and serve someone who is worse off than you. Do something to get outside of yourself. There is a power to be found when you help others and also in simply forgetting about yourself for a while.

Of course, some people need medication to jumpstart the brain after six months or more of depression, so they can achieve a brain chemistry that's receptive to learning more effective coping mechanisms. However, acute depression is usually the result of nothing more than *looking at things the wrong way*. If you recognize the pattern, you can put a different energy out there and stop doing it.

An attitude of weakness typically will attract more people who are weak around you. Changing your focus changes your life. You'll attract a different reality. That's the potential danger of support groups, in which people spend their time lamenting and sharing their problems. There is a risk of getting mired in the problems and never moving forward. It becomes the way you define your life. More importantly, it shapes your expectations. Support groups should actually go to *serve* others to get a dose of reality by comparison and the strength that comes in helping another.

This is especially true with our baggage from childhood. Many people spend their entire lives blaming their parents for where they are now. They feel unequipped to deal with life in the present and they blame their parents. Or they are so consumed with anger and bitterness that they make their parents the scapegoat. The psychological term is learned helplessness—believing that something or someone else holds the power to your happiness, your success or whatever it may be, and that whatever you do is futile.

In reality, the answer to all of our problems is right here in front of us—in *the now*, not back in childhood, but back to utopia! The challenge is for us to yield to our weaknesses and become who we are by overcoming them. After all, what are you going to do? Change your DNA? Change your history? Does a zebra wake up and say, *"How did I get these stripes?"* Zebras don't ask those questions—we're the ones with choice and logic and emotion, *and we're also the ones with issues!*

We have the power of choice and decision and that's where the challenge is. We all have weakness; however, we also all have the key to greatness and strength if we know how to transform that weakness. Like the caterpillar changing structures to become a butterfly, we can become *great* out of our worst experiences and shortcomings.

TURN YOUR LOWS UPSIDE DOWN

The greater a person's weakness is, the more potential there is for a height of equal greatness. If the valley is deep then the mountain is high! A valley is nothing more than an inverted mountain. When we're in a "pit," we think, *"How can life get any worse at this moment?"* The alchemy of weakness to greatness is a constant mind game of changing our perception.

There are some periods of weakness where you can pick yourself up by the bootstraps and just change it. However, you could have missed an opportunity to learn from that space of weakness, rather than just get out of it. There are times when weakness is the greatest kind of learning.

Retired Admiral Jim Stockdale, who you may remember as Ross Perot's running mate in the 1992 presidential election, was a prisoner of war for eight years during the Vietnam War. Years later, he said it was the best thing that ever happened to him because it showed him what life was really about. When asked what distinguished him from the men who didn't make it, he responded that he took every day *one day at a time*, rather than living for the future. The men who died in prison were the ones who gave themselves a timeline, an expectation of when they'd get out, such as Christmas or Easter. Admiral Stockdale survived not by focusing on better days ahead, but on today. He always had faith that everything would turn out ok, and also encouraged his fellow inmates, but he also accepted the harsh circumstances of his reality. He lived in the now!

If you have the power to change something from weakness to strength, change it quickly so you don't get stuck. But accept that there are some things you can't change. Some weaknesses you have no control over. You have to allow that tragedy or weakness to train you, like my son's disability. I finally got to that point after three years of agony, wondering how can I make this better or what's wrong with me, and I realized I had to embrace his weakness to best help him. I had to stop thinking about myself and maximize my weakness to serve him. I finally said, *It is what it is and I'm weak only if I allow this to beat me.*

I had the built-in gift of my son. I had to unwrap it every day, and I didn't have time to focus on all my issues. That's the power of allowing your weakness to educate you. Embrace it and serve it. That's "The Gift" of weakness.

Chapter 4
Crisis Is the Toughness Chamber

"Life's not what it's supposed to be. It's what it is.
The way you cope with it is what makes the difference."
– Virginia Satir

I believe from my own life experience and the experiences of the people I've helped over the years that *crisis is what drives us to change*. Real change takes place only with crisis because we're too comfortable with the way things are, even when they're bad. No one likes change—we like things left alone.

A crisis can be defined as the ultimate stress, which is the stimulus for all action and growth. Today, many of us are crashing into our personal and professional lives because we're trying to avoid crisis. We're trying to defy the gravity of a life stress that we have little control over. I deal with this every day. People say, "*I don't know how much longer I can take this*," or, "*The stress from my job/life/kids/marriage is killing me.*" They want to wish it all away, rather than discovering the lessons crisis has to offer.

If you really want to grow, you have to learn to embrace crisis. The stories of crisis are the same for all of us, even though the faces may change. It doesn't matter how weird or terrible you think a problem is; it's your *response* to the situation that

40

defines you. As people, we can learn to work within the natural laws of gravity—we can use gravity to help us soar to new levels of excellence. When I say there's an opportunity in crisis, what I mean is let's not look for what's wrong here, but for the opportunity. It's all about flipping that coin. Viewing life's stresses as a challenge, rather than a threat, is a matter of changing your perspective.

Ultimately, any situation in your life that you wish would go away is a real "toughness chamber." It's an opportunity to show yourself what you're made of, which can toughen you and prepare you for the rest of your life. Evolution is a process of change that continually happens over the course of every person's life. Transitions are the necessary periods of adjustment between evolutions. As a result, a transition is the most difficult time in our life because it whips us out of one evolution and into another. A crisis can be looked at as nothing more than a *transition*.

The "toughness chamber" of crisis, however, requires us to recognize the difference between being tough and being hardened. Life toughness is made up of three factors: strength, flexibility and resiliency. *Strength* is the ability to dig deep and stand firm in the midst of crisis. *Flexibility* is the ability to quickly change and adapt to life's circumstances. *Resilience* is the ability to keep coming back until you succeed.

Flexibility is the most difficult trait of the three to develop and maintain. You can be strong and you can be resilient, but you must be *flexible* to truly succeed. Think of an athlete: a physically strong athlete without flexibility is an athlete ready for injury. The same principle applies to mental flexibility. Effectively responding to a crisis requires toughness, without hardness. If you are hard, you are inflexible.

Crisis gives us the ability to become elastic and learn that flexibility!

Usually, what toughens us are the things that go wrong in our lives. As John Lennon said, "Life is what happens while you're busy making other plans." Most people have their lives figured out. They have two kids, a house, a career and they can see the long road ahead of them. Then gravity hits—a crisis they never saw coming—and they're required to be flexible.

It is our degree of toughness that determines how well we emerge from a crisis. Success doesn't mean that we never get overwhelmed or fall apart or feel like giving up. Success means we pick ourselves up one more time than we are knocked down.

FROM SURVIVING TO THRIVING

When a crisis hits, we go into survival mode. This is the natural, temporary first step in dealing with any crisis. Survival mode is similar to automatic pilot; the body's fight-or-flight mechanism is activated and it focuses us on what we must do to stay alive, right now. Survival mode is an unconscious response mechanism that helps us respond to a threat or danger.

At 9:00 a.m. on September 11, 2001, no one in the World Trade Center was worried about the stock market or the economy. No one was thinking about his 401(k) or her upcoming vacation. At that moment, those people were focused on one thing: getting out of those buildings. In survival mode, we act first, then think. It's a reflex. We don't have to actually touch the fire before the response kicks in and jerks our hand away from the flame.

Unfortunately, some people get stuck in survival mode and it begins to take its toll on mind and body. Fight-or-flight is designed to be a temporary response. People who stay in survival mode are the ones who end up with anxiety disorders, panic attacks, depression, distractibility issues, and weight gain, in addition to suffering compromised immune systems and, ultimately, disease.

We need to go beyond *survival mode* into a *thriving mode*. I can appreciate when a crisis happens because I know there's something good for me. Functioning is the state between surviving and thriving, and it's how most people live on a daily basis. People who function handle the daily challenges of life with a fair degree of balance. They hold an even keel, they earn a living, they raise their children, they get involved in their communities. Life is good. The drawback of the function mode is that people expend so much energy functioning, they have little left to meet their full potential.

Those who *thrive* represent the upper echelon of achievement and performance, consistently about 1% of people. This is where the elite live—the elite performers, athletes, military members and entrepreneurs who deliver excellence consistently, in every area of their life. Instead of pulling back from a challenge, these people thrive by learning to fall forward and embrace challenge. They know that feeling pain or discomfort doesn't necessarily mean they've reached their limit. Pain is a natural stimulus that is a normal by-product of any process of growth and development. Thriving requires us to fall into pain, knowing it will only make us stronger.

Friedrich Nietzsche said, "That which does not kill us makes us stronger." It's true, but only if you learn from crisis by submitting to it.

THE POWER OF A "MOCK" CRISIS

Sometimes, a "mock crisis" can help show us what we are capable of so we make changes to create a better life. I recommend this all the time in life coaching when a client is confronted with what feels like an unbearable life stress. For instance, I might say to someone struggling with stress at home: "*I want you to pull onto the side of the road on your way home from work today, and turn off the radio and just sit there. Next, I want you to visualize walking into the house and finding your spouse and children dead. I want you to see, hear, feel and touch it. Experience it to the point that it moves you. When it does, come back to yourself and calmly drive home and re-experience your family for the first time.*"

It sounds harsh, but 9 times out of 10, the person goes home and has a whole new outlook on their family. The mock crisis works off of the old saying, "*You don't know what you have until it's gone.*" You can create this awareness mentally before tragedy hits, enabling you to actually salvage that relationship or situation successfully.

I personally did this with my son, Brandon, for many years. I would reach my breaking point and think, "*I just can't go without sleep again and get up for work or go to school.*" So, I would do this exercise. I would imagine him gone and, as morbid as it sounds, it made me appreciate him and my life, not the scenarios around my life. It realigned my priorities and was very powerful.

In life, there is no greater crisis than losing someone you love. Grief is a transitional state between past reality and future reality, and crisis is nothing more than the trigger for that grief. Crisis is truly the great equalizer in life—we're all going to experience it, regardless of age, sex, religion or beliefs. However, the good news is that, as I said in the beginning of this book, we're all wired for crisis. Birth is our first and biggest crisis, and we survived it.

MY BROTHER'S GIFT

Several years ago, my brother, Roger, passed away from cancer as a result of AIDS. He was gay and I wasn't very close to him for much of our adult lives. We talked maybe once a year. This was long before gay rights, and when growing up, I never understood Roger because I liked women. I thought being gay was weird, but now I wonder: what's normal? We're all weird, and we try to make other people like us, instead of acquiescing to and learning from others.

One day, my mother called and said she had something to tell me. I asked what. She said, "*Your brother is gay,*" and I'm thinking, "*You just figured this out?*" But then she went on to say, "*And he has HIV.*"

I went to visit Roger shortly after the diagnosis and he was shocked to see me walk in the door. He asked what I was doing there, and I said mom had called and told me what was going on. I told him that even though we'd never had a close relationship, I was here for him and willing to do whatever he needed. He was very surprised, but accepted my olive branch.

It started a really interesting period in our relationship that would last for the next three years. I learned a lot in the process. I submitted to his crisis and learned to be a servant to him. He got to know my boys and they him. Brent and Brandon loved him just like an aunt, which is what he was! They adored him.

As Roger's health worsened, it was very difficult to watch him get ill and die in front of my eyes. But it was gravity; it was going to happen. Roger told me before he died that he didn't want me to speak at his funeral, knowing I had never understood his lifestyle. Eventually, he did pass away and though I wasn't there with him the moment he died, I knew we had mended our relationship.

When we opened the will, we were shocked to see that Roger had crossed out a paragraph and added, in his own writing, that he wanted me to do the eulogy at his funeral. It shocked me and showed me that he trusted me as his brother, who would do the right thing and say what mattered most in memory of his life. I did Roger's eulogy, just like my dad's. I remember standing up there in front of 75 gay men, friends and family, commemorating Roger's life. I realized I was able to share how much Roger taught me about diversity and about things I never understood.

And though it was also agonizing to watch my brother die, it was a time of significant growth and change that I'll never forget. I was glad that Roger was free of his pain, and that his crisis, even something as horrible as AIDS, could become an opportunity to inform and enrich my life.

There is so much controversy to this day about gay rights, and I respect Roger's choice. He died living what he believed in—which is more than I could say for myself at the time. If it weren't for Roger's crisis, I may never have come to love him and understand him as I did.

INSULATION VS ISOLATION

When I was in Thailand working with tsunami victims, I traveled for a day to refugee camps a bit south of where I was working. The camp was a large field with military tents and holding areas for homeless families and individuals. The man I had traveled with, David, a forensic doctor and freelance photographer from Turkey, walked past some of the open tents. Inside, children were painting pictures of their experiences during the tsunami. Their paintings, hung up on clotheslines to dry, were colorful expressions of their emotional and mental stress. They were amazing: imaginative depictions of the great wall of water covering houses, boats and trees, and skies filled with birds escaping the watery grave below.

The children were being overseen by a group of Japanese relief workers. I asked one young woman who spoke English to convey to the other workers what a wonderful idea I thought the painting exercise was for the children's healing process. The paintings allowed the children to release the stress and trauma trapped inside, and to vent their toxic memories of the disaster, clearing the way for healing and recovery.

The story brings up an important point, in addition to emphasizing the importance of properly recovering from stress: how we raise our children to handle life's storms, both literally and metaphorically, can train them to thrive or merely survive.

There is a difference between *insulating* children from the harshness of daily life and *isolating* them. Healthy parenting is about insulation: giving your kids the awareness, tools and strategies to effectively navigate life. You let them skin their knees and deal with common stresses, like sibling rivalry or typical peer experiences, without solving it for them. Parents who are overprotective, on the other hand, isolate their children from these necessary learning experiences.

Isolation causes kids to unravel when confronted with life, because they haven't built up enough toughness through their own process of trial and error. They haven't confronted enough gravity to learn from it and effectively respond to it.

Ray Evernham, founder and CEO of Gillett Evernham Motorsports, currently in his seventh full season at the helm of one of NASCAR's premier racing organizations, almost burned to death in a racecar during his own driving career. Fortunately, he was able to run across the track with his arm burning because of the fire insulation he had on underneath his race suit.

Evernham's story is also a metaphor for dealing with crisis: every day, prepare for the worst, but expect the best. In Evernham's case, he didn't have time to go find his firesuit once his car caught on fire; he already had it on. That's why I believe in good stress—it insulates us from life. A person's performance, in life and in everything, is only going to be as good as his preparation. If we isolate our kids from stress and solve all of their problems for them, we're going to deprive them of the experiences that produce life toughness.

Kids are stronger than we think. They're *wired* for success. It's society and many well-intentioned parents' exaggerated fears or need for control that *programs* them for failure by not allowing them to learn the necessary skills to navigate through life. While we always want to protect and nurture our children, we also want to allow stress to be the positive force it can be. Stress is gravity: we can't escape it, so we must learn as early as possible how to work with it.

In helping our children deal with stress, it is helpful to teach them that everything happens for a reason. This will enable them, as it does us, to come to grips with many things that can't be explained or fully understood. It is also important to prepare them for the understanding that life will not always be easy. The sooner they learn this and the sooner they learn to process stress as a powerful *positive* force in their lives, the healthier and happier they will become. It will help them be better equipped to deal with crisis in their lives later on.

For people of any age, stress is a potential stimulus for healthy growth. Falling forward into stress and crisis eases us through the doors of opportunities. We are falling forward when we lean into success that is not yet seen, but only believed in. The more we learn to deal with crisis, the stronger we will become and the more our capacities will expand beyond their limits. Because of this, crisis is "The Gift."

As you look at this photo, ask yourself the question: Are you the comforted or the comforter? Life offers us opportunity to do both. If we're only one or the other, we're missing life. Those who are only comforters cannot receive; they're unhealthy caretakers and enablers. Those who can't comfort are narcissistic takers, which is equally unhealthy. We need to become both the comforter and the comforted in our lives. The gift is crisis.

Chapter 5
Failure Is A Lesson

"The thing that is really hard and really amazing is giving up on being perfect and beginning the work of becoming yourself."
– Anna Quindlen

Failure knocks us down and we can move forward or backward, depending on how we respond. Failure basically means we prove to be unsuccessful. However, there are very few failures in life; most failures are lessons we are still learning.

Failure is not a finality, rather, a learning opportunity. If you can apply what you learn and do something with it, you've transformed a failure into an advantage. I remind myself of *failing forward* when I fail—as long as I *fail forward*, I'm six feet closer to my goal. If I don't, nothing positive comes of my failure. Like most people, I've failed more in my life than I've succeeded, but because I can learn from my failures, I've grown. I've made something out of the life experiences that many of us perceive as a waste of time or a loss.

When most people fail, they believe they're in a negative position compared to when they began. But if you flip that coin and realize failing isn't the issue, but rather not *learning* from the failure, you'll actually be richer in life experience afterwards. There is no law that says you must be in a loss position after you fail.

If anything, you're more equipped to move ahead and excel.

Thomas Edison, the inventor of the first commercially viable light bulb, once said: "I've not failed. I've just learned 10,000 ways that won't work." Can you imagine if he had given up? If he had perceived his failures as confirmation of his own shortcomings or of the unworthiness of his goal? Edison took his failures as learning experiences and they eventually led him to one of the most important inventions of the 19th century!

Today, a similar attitude toward failure can be seen in modern-day researchers, scientists, entrepreneurs and athletes. These are the men and women who use every one of their life experiences to propel them forward. They squeeze the last drop of potential from everything that's happened in their lives, so that every moment—even the failures—are a positive.

Michael Jordan was cut from his high school basketball team. Steve Jobs, co-founder of Apple, was fired from the company in 1985, only to return 12 years later as its CEO! Oprah Winfrey overcame every obstacle a person can think of—social, economical, psychological and physical—to become a living legend of inspiration. When we hear the stories of great people's lives, their failures have a way of paving the way to their ultimate success. Failure is part of the "story" of where they've come from and where they're going.

The great moments and inventions of the 20th century have come from people who *grew from their failures, instead of being limited by them*. And we're no different! Every person has greatness inside them that can be molded and strengthened by failure. In fact, true character is forged in these moments of crisis and failure. The more life challenges you confront and the more you respond with an attitude of learning, the more you will develop yourself as a person.

Later, we'll talk about how part of performance is measured in the speed of recovery—it's not how far or how often you fall, but how quickly you get up. A racecar driver will drive into a wall at 200 miles per hour, and jump back into the backup car and do it all over again the next day. Toddlers fall, get patched up and are on their way again before they even know what hit them. They're not petrified or traumatized. A child keeps going, over and over again, because they have good recovery speed. They bounce back.

We're all wired to learn from our failures. We're wired for success, but *programmed for failure*. It's inevitable that we will fail sometime in life, but what we can control is our response to those failures. Are you going to avoid life? Are you going to stop taking risks? Every part of life is a minefield of potential failures: parenting, starting a new business, dating, loving, snowboarding, investing in the stock market and even something as simple as driving your car! If you think you failed one time, you may not try again. But if you think you learned from the experience, you will try again. Every one of us can learn this lesson.

Failing forward is an attitude, a mentality. You choose to do something with a failure, to move forward and make something of it. Failure is learning, uniquely disguised as failure.

FEAR OF FAILING

I had a day of awakening when I was finishing school and coaching a person who was having some serious personal problems. I remember sitting there thinking, *"This person really needs to be talking to someone!"* Then it hit me, *"Hello! You're that person...the only other person in the room!"* And I really had to dig deep and be that source of guidance for him, and trust that my advice wouldn't create more problems than he already had. I now consider that moment to be the beginning of my professional career.

Looking back, I realize that I was willing to take the risk, step up to the plate and do my job. I was ready for possible failure and what I would learn from it, though I may not have been able to verbalize it at the time. We all have to reach that mindset in which we are willing to fail, because we know our progress depends on it. Failure that's learned from gives us the confidence to teach and mentor others in our lives. No one has infinite knowledge, and part of the journey is minimizing the expectation that we should be perfect before we teach others. We're going to move towards that level of knowledge and confidence we seek by jumping in, helping others and, inevitably, failing some of the time.

They say that those who can't do, teach. Maybe there is some truth to this statement, but teaching is one of the greatest deeds in life—to give back to someone and help them because of your experience. We're all teachers, with our own set of life "expertise" that's been born out of our successes and failures. Ultimately, it's not about being perfect. It's about trying to become more complete, through helping others and making sense of our failures.

The good-enough school of teaching applies nowhere more powerfully than to parenting. Most parents agree that being a parent is the hardest job in the world. No matter how many books you've read, nothing prepares you. You're going to make mistakes and see yourself in your children's failures. Your kids are going to learn from you and repeat many of your failures. Along with the indescribable love and joys of parenting comes a heavy burden that your guidance, for better and for worse, is eternally shaping a child's life.

I remember when I came to grips with the fact that my son, Brandon, was never going to talk or walk in his life. It was a stark reality when I came to this realization. We were getting Brandon fitted for his orthotics to help him function as much as possible in his state. The word orthotics comes form the root "ortho," which means "to straighten." The orthotics were not going to fix Brandon, but they would be there to support him and his body as much as possible for optimal function. Brandon's life wasn't over; it was just slower because of his special needs. Like any failure, the solution wasn't to fix it, but allow it to help and teach us how to be the best we could moving forward.

Whether a wheelchair or a bankruptcy, life isn't over. It's altered and, if you respond correctly, supported by the failure. Some of us have physical failures and others of us have professional or personal failures. *We are all special needs people.* My needs are different than yours, but we all have our areas that need support. There are many people walking around who don't know that.

The ability to extract the necessary support structures from our failures is what strengthens us and allows us to continue living.

FAILURE IS NOW, NOT ALWAYS

When we personalize a failure, we generalize it.
Actually, we only failed in one situation and often we
simply didn't have the proper information in that
circumstance.

The truth is that the majority of people process life
from pain, not from comfort. A fear of failure can start
to paralyze a person's life, if they believe they can't
handle pain or won't bounce back from a failure. But
we have to be unafraid of failure to succeed. Thank
goodness Edison or the Wright Brothers weren't
afraid of failing. Sometimes, it can look strange when
a person says, *"I'm not going to get discouraged by a
failure; I'm going to keep trying."* It looks bizarre to the
outside observer, who may be calculating a tight risk-
benefit formula and conclude it's unwise to continue
risking for so little in return. However, to the great
person, there is no question they're going to do it
again. They're not going to let the attempt-failure
define them as a personal failure.

Any of the greats will tell you they learned more from
their failures than their successes. It wasn't easy to
get where they are and there were many bumps along
the way, which were necessary to their ultimate
success.

Failure could be the greatest schoolmaster we have, if we use it correctly. We simply need to allow it to *school* us and not *defeat* us.

SUCCESS NEEDS FAILURE

Without failure, success is never fully understood or appreciated. Today, we have such misguided beliefs about success. Many people think if you make a lot of money, if you're on TV, or if you look a certain way, you're a success. In reality, this isn't success at all. Success is an attitude, not a destination or a possession. Success comes from inside a person, not from the envious gaze of others.

The trap of mistaking success for what it's not is common in people who achieve success early. Young athletes and celebrities make all kinds of money, and achieve the fame and attention they believe is supposed to make them happy. But you only need to look as far as the latest celebrity downfall story to realize that success in its superficial terms is not all it's cracked up to be. Young and old alike, people tend to make terrible decisions when they achieve such "success" because they start to think they're special. They think the rules of life don't apply to them and they stop appreciating life's gifts.

In contrast, the celebrities and athletes with balance— who keep working hard and know they're no different than anyone else—are the ones who do well and achieve lasting (and authentic) success. These also happen to be the people who can handle and embrace failure, without self-destructing or peaking before their time.

Ultimately, famous or not, we are all equals! No one is better than anyone else and usually, the sooner we realize this, the better our life tends to go. Normal is what you see in the mirror every day. Many of us look at ourselves and say, *"That's it!"* And we look at others and say, *"They're weird,"* or *"They're inferior."* We're all weird and we're all built from the same basic wiring. The question is: Are you at grips with your own weirdness and shortcomings? That understanding really comes out of understanding failure. One of the greatest lessons I've learned from my son, Brandon, is that whatever height I've reached, I still serve from a valley that he resides in.

FAILING FROM THE HEART

Harnessing the power of failure also means that you know when to continue in spite of failure and when to put your energy and resources in another direction. For someone who fails repeatedly and feels sorry for themselves, I would ask them: *"Are you failing at same thing over and over again?"* Usually, this indicates you have not learned "the lesson" and passed "the test." Life will test you to develop what you need, and if you fail, life will continue presenting the problem to you over and over again until you find your way through. It is magical thinking to believe that life or the universe *has it out for you*. You're in charge and your response controls the outcome.

Trying to reach the same goal and repeatedly failing also happens to be the definition of insanity, to paraphrase Benjamin Franklin. Unless you are taking a different tactic or re-envisioning what you desire, expecting it to happen when you continue taking the same action is, well, crazy. Or, it could be that you're trying too many approaches and need to try to achieve one thing at a time. Simplify to whittle away at failure.

However, this advice takes us back to the many great men and women who tried and tried and tried…and succeeded at last. They looked crazy. They may have been crazy. But they reached the pinnacle ultimately. The gamble of where they were putting their resources, sometimes for a lifetime, paid off. But there is no guarantee, and risking your life for a goal you may never achieve is risky. This applies whether the goal is a job, a love or a personal ideal. The risk is proportionate to how much of your life energy you devote to achieving the goal, which can be either the reward or the price at the end of it.

Deciding when failure is a signpost to keep going and when it's a warning to stop is a highly personal decision that *each person has to make for themselves*. Another great man, Abraham Lincoln, failed multiple times in running for public office before he was elected as President of the United States. It's another example of believing, "*I'm not failing; this is my destiny.*" The line between insanity and destiny is listening to your heart. Are you connected to a strong sense that your destiny is calling and it's supposed to be this way? Or are you avoiding real work or real relationships by aiming for something so high and, in all likelihood, so unrealistic? Only you can answer that question and you are the one who has to live with the consequences.

Every person needs that confidence, and inner sense of strength and guidance to lead them along the right path in life. The prospect of failure can become an easy excuse at both ends of the spectrum: you get too familiar with failure and think it's all life has to offer you, *or* you stop living your life because you fear failure. Either way, that's how you get trapped. You allow failure to *fail you* by giving into the failure and giving up. Go inside yourself and ask yourself the hard questions.

I believe that if you have enough belief in yourself, ultimately, nothing is going to stop you and no goal is unattainable. I tell people on a regular basis: you can resign your job every day or leave a bad relationship, but people who believe in what they want won't *quit easily*. Resigning simply means you're frustrated, but you haven't given up. If you really do what you love, often the money will follow. If you really want a healthy, mutually loving relationship, you'll find it. You get up, dust yourself off and continue putting one foot in front of the other, day after day. Otherwise, you'll be a slave to money or a slave to someone else—and you'll blame it on everyone else, except yourself!

The greatest formula for success is *not giving up*. That's it! Know in your bones that this is what you're supposed to be doing, and you're already on your way. Two-thirds of life's journey is not quitting. If you can learn from your failures, you can convert those experiences into success. Failure is "The Gift."

Chapter 6
Follow Your Pain

*"History, despite its wrenching pain, cannot be unlived,
but if faced with courage, need not be lived again."*
– Maya Angelou

Pain is our friend. Pain is nothing more than an emotional response to something that's gone wrong. Without the pain sensors in our body, we would literally run ourselves to death. Pain is an indicator that protects us from the injury that can occur from life.

Pain is nothing more than a symptom; it's not actually the problem. Pain is a secondary alarm saying *something else* is wrong. It's up to us to use our logic and life experience to interpret that pain, then identify and eliminate the root of it to avoid causing injury to ourselves or others.

Most people don't try to eliminate the source of their pain. They either do something superficial to temporarily numb it or they get used to the pain. They learn to *function* with pain, but not *thrive*. They tell themselves this is the way it is. When you don't deal with the source of your pain, you never learn nor heal from it. You therefore never reach your full potential, because some (or all) of your energy is going towards tolerating pain, rather than eliminating it.

65

Pain is the result of what I call the Dagger Syndrome—there is a source to the pain you're experiencing and it's what holds the key to your recovery. You know you have a dagger in your gut, but until you pull it out, that pain is never going to go away. The problem is the dagger. The pain receptors in that area are saying: *"Pay attention to me! Something is wrong here!"* If you don't deal with the source of your pain, it eventually creates a situation in which you are walking around with a dagger in your gut and you know no different because this is now your reality!

The source of pain can become obscure over time, when you've become accustomed to living with it. But intuitively or through a life crisis, many people know that they are not functioning as well as they could be. They are not living their best life. I help people identify their pain and find that dagger, so relief and healing can take place.

Pain can be in any of our capacities as individuals: mental, emotional, spiritual, or physical. In fact, there is a very fine line between these four dimensions, and pain in one capacity can leak into another. They are all interconnected and support each other. I only need one leak in my boat to eventually begin a process of expending time, effort, and energy into bailing water instead of spending that same effort into the journey and the destination. If I have a recurring mental pain issue—such as negative self-talk or a bad vision of myself—that can bleed over to show up as emotional pain or spiritual pain. I can become depressed or doubt that I will ever be anything or that my life means anything. So a mental "dagger" creates pain, not just mentally, but emotionally and spiritually, too. My confidence and larger belief system are shaken, and, if I'm not careful, this can create illness, too, affecting the fourth capacity (the physical).

Most people think of pain as emotional or physical in nature, but mental and spiritual pain exists, too. All four capacities inside of us must thrive to create flow in our lives. Discovering the *dagger*, or the root of our pain, in one capacity restores balance mentally, emotionally, spiritually and physically, for our best life.

FOUR KINDS OF PAIN

Pain is a stimulus that we can grow from. When something is causing us discomfort, that pain can be a stimulus for growth, since we are challenging ourselves to find a new way of functioning.

As I said in the opening of this chapter, there are four dimensions we operate in as human beings and, consequently, there are four types of pain: mental, emotional, spiritual and physical.

Physical pain is the most tangible pain. We can directly feel it and, in some cases, see it. We know when a health condition, like back pain, is affecting how we function. We know how breaking a bone in our body limits our mobility. However, it may be less obvious to us how that physical pain affects our thought process or our faith in ourselves. Some people begin to identify with their physical condition to the point that it becomes their *identity*. Even in the case of a chronic health condition, which may not be solved physically, it's important to assess whether we are carrying around a mental or emotional dagger related to that condition. Tackling the reality of that pain head-on, rather than using it as a crutch or a cop-out in other areas of life, is important. Physical pain doesn't encapsulate who you are. You still exist in other dimensions independent of that pain, and it's important to continue nourishing yourself mentally, emotionally and spiritually in spite of physical pain.

Emotional pain is equally familiar to most people. We know when we feel sad or depressed or regretful. We often feel these emotions in the context of a relationship, with friends, family, loved ones and colleagues. A common example of emotional pain is dealing with a difficult person at work that you can't fire. Since you can't quit, you have to learn to adapt and deal with the person, which ultimately creates growth in *you if you understand and utilize it correctly*.

While our relationships may appear to be the root of our emotional pain, it's actually our *response* that controls the pain we're experiencing. As adults, we *allow* other people to affect us. Part of managing emotional pain is realizing that another person's behavior doesn't have to dictate how you feel. You are in charge of your feelings. If someone influences you to feel badly about yourself or frustrated, you're going to find the answer by changing *your* behavior, not theirs.

Mental and spiritual pain are less defined than physical and emotional pain. A good example of mental pain is the process of schooling. Getting an education stretches the mind through studying, reading and test-taking. We're asked to go outside of what we know and expand our knowledge base. School creates mental stress that benefits you, *if* you rise to the occasion instead of avoiding it.

Forging new relationships is another example of mental stress. New people require us to change the way we interact and, often, our expectations and beliefs. How many times have you met someone you didn't like at first, only to become great friends (or more) later? Your initial dislike was an example of mental pain, created by your unfamiliarity. By sticking it out and getting to know the person, you expanded your belief system and added value to your life.

Spiritual pain is the least tangible type of pain, but it can be the most profound in terms of its impact on our life. I experienced a deep spiritual pain for several years, when I somehow believed that God would fix my son, Brandon. I took him to churches and prayed for him, believing that some form of divine intervention eventually would heal him. This belief caused a huge amount of spiritual pain for me, because each day it didn't happen, I would wonder how there could be a just and loving God who would do this to me. I created a spiritual pain in my life. Eventually, I was able to alleviate my pain by not putting all of my hope in the healing, but in the belief that if God chose not to heal Brandon, I would grow from it and go on to be able to help people, and that is exactly what happened. The dagger was my mistaken hope that by believing in God, my son would automatically be healed. This would have left me happy, but shallow regarding life and helping others in pain.

Many people think that pain is just what it is—pain. But really, we only need to change our vision. Maybe there is a purpose to our pain or a lesson hidden there to teach us, but we're too busy being blinded by the pain. Many things in the world seem unfair. There are starving people living in poverty, abused children and many smaller issues of life's unfairness. However, instead of becoming full of rage, hate or numbness, we must stop living in an element of pain we feel helpless over. I still hurt and cry to this day about my son's situation, after 22 years. It's just no longer my obsession. My focus is making sure I can be as healthy as possible and making Brandon as healthy as possible, even in the midst of this pain that is recurring and never going to end.

Pain can be our friend if we learn from it. Flipping that coin is what reveals pain's lesson and provides us some relief in the process. Anything in a prolonged state of pain (whether mental, emotional, spiritual or physical) can create injury. We don't grow from injury; we recover from it. So the balance is identifying the source of our pain and removing it, but also recognizing that some pain isn't solvable. We simply have to live with it, in the best way we can.

Pain is the great equalizer. None of us are immune to it. I believe that those who have a high tolerance to pain, in most cases, have a deeper level of endured pain in their life that they've learned from. It allows them to say, "*I've felt worse than this; I'm not dying.*" Other people experience a very minor amount of pain and they bleed out emotionally. Everyone's ability to tolerate pain is different, but we're all going to experience pain. Each of us needs to learn to master the processing of pain, so we move forward. Usually, the experience of *prior* pain is the best way to learn the necessary flexibility and resilience to move through *future* pain.

WRITE A LETTER

A great step in dealing with pain is to write letters about someone or something that has caused you pain. The first step in dealing with pain is assessing whether the pain is still active or not. In other words, *if*

there is pain, it is still a wound, and if not, it is a scar!
A wound still requires attention. A scar has healed
and become part of you. If you can touch a spot in
yourself mentally, emotionally, spiritually or physically
and it still hurts, that's a wound. If you can think of
someone who hurt you without feeling pain, it's a
scar. You've forgiven or moved on and it's not going
to cause you further pain and injury. *Pain is what
differentiates a wound from a scar.*

In psychology, the venting process is known as
catharsis. You visit a therapist to unload thoughts,
emotions, memories and baggage from the past to
make room for new ways of thinking, feeling and
connecting. You're purging yourself of injury by
sorting through that pain.

When I train students, I describe catharsis as
emotional puking. As gross as that sounds, you get
the picture, especially if you are on the receiving end
of the mess. Trained people insulate themselves like
wearing protective clothing. But lacking this training
will leave the recipient smelling badly. Worse yet, they
get used to the smell and then act like nothing is
wrong. This can cause bitterness and pain that will be
acted out on others later, thus becoming an
emotionally sick person replaying this scenario on
others.

Writing letters to someone who has caused you pain
or writing about a painful experience offers a similar

exercise in catharsis. You get your thoughts, feelings and memories onto paper. Then you destroy the letters, doing it over and over until you don't feel the need to write any longer. It's inexpensive therapy and it works.

Many people worry that if they "stir things up" in their mind, they'll be overwhelmed with bad feelings and memories. But the reality is that these mental and emotional daggers are *already in there*. You're not creating them. You're finally uprooting them and freeing yourself for a healthier, happier life. We only have a finite amount of energy. When unfinished business lurks under the surface, we devote our energy to that rather than to what we want in life, often without even realizing it.

Don't be shy or put limits on yourself. It may take you 100 letters or it may take you one letter, but you'll know when that dagger has been dislodged and healing can begin, because the pain will disappear.

TEACH YOUR CHILDREN WELL

As I'll say many times throughout this book, the most important lessons in life tend to be learned during childhood. We can always change and grow later on, but the more a parent is able to guide a child right during the formative years, the more easily that child will transition into adulthood equipped to deal with life.

Parenting is a delicate balance of allowing a child to grow and also putting boundaries around that child to ensure that development is happening in a way that supports future health, happiness and success.

Physical discipline of children gets a bad rap in today's child-centric culture. A whole generation has been raised without much discipline because psychologists and pediatricians told parents it would make a child violent or harm their development. But after seeing the effects of children who grew up without discipline—a lack of respect for elders, trouble differentiating as self-sufficient adults and not even knowing themselves—I believe that people who aren't disciplined when young will have lower levels of self-discipline later.

Some parents avoid physical discipline because they see it as cruel and barbaric. They believe it's teaching a child to be violent, instead of imparting a lesson. But violence is embedded in our DNA. It's a survival instinct and, if anything, we're tempering children's natural tendency towards aggression and violence when we discipline them.

In fact, abuse is the opposite of discipline and discipline is not abuse. Discipline is scolding for the good of the child, while abuse is acting to release your own anger and aggression. My mom used to say when she spanked me, "*This is going to hurt me more than it hurts you*," and at the time I thought, "*No way.*"

But as I've grown and had my own children, I realize it probably did. That pain helped prevent a future injury in me.

Instilling some degree of disciplinary pain in a child's life can help protect them from more pain in the future. Training up a child to be a good, empowered and healthy person is always going to involve some pain. It's like that pain of learning in school or in a new relationship that we talked about earlier. The child is literally learning to expand their sense of the world and themselves. It's a growing process, and growing sometimes hurts.

Healthy discipline in childhood creates good self-discipline later on. *The goal of proper discipline is to protect the spirit of a child—not break it.* Breaking the spirit is abuse. Discipline allows the spirit to thrive by helping the child learn to rein in his or her will, so they can become thriving people in adulthood. Happy, productive adults have good self-discipline, a big part of which is having good boundaries around ourselves, so we aren't abused or taken advantage of by others.

Healthy discipline is another example of how pain can be helpful and beneficial. Few people understand the value of proper discipline and how to apply it correctly. Form a child in development, and you'll shape who they are for the rest of their lives. You can teach pain to be your child's friend, if it's used as an educational tool to train them how to live life and *do* life with others, not just themselves. When children learn to submit to a measured and healthy amount of pain, they're prepared to stretch their minds, put up with difficult people and check their belief systems as adults.

LAUGHTER IS GREAT MEDICINE

I talked about writing letters as one of the quickest, easiest ways to transition through pain or, for children, to have them draw pictures about their thoughts and feelings, then throw them away.

Another great way to process pain is through laughter. Think of a young child, who gets angry or hurts himself from falling down. Usually, if you start laughing, they will stop crying and start laughing, too. They'll be fine, almost as if by magic. You've changed their focus from the pain or upset they're feeling to something brighter in life.

Laughter is a great antidote to pain at all ages. What person doesn't want a relationship they can laugh in? Most people want to be with someone who is caring, loving, sensual, sexy and also *funny*—a person who can laugh at themselves and with other people, with a warm sense of humor. And what's worse than someone with no sense of humor? Usually these are the people who are so uptight they can't laugh themselves. Or, they're bullies who berate others, but can't take it in return.

The majority of comedians have come from a background with a great deal of pain. They learned how to deal with pain by laughing and making others laugh. They flipped the coin by finding the humor in life. Laughter became the antidote, and while it may not have cured the pain, it helped them deal with it.

Laughter does a lot. A key aspect of dealing with pain is learning to laugh at ourselves and simply take it all less seriously. Laughter releases endorphins, those feel-good chemicals in the brain. Studies have found that laughing for just a few minutes a day reduces blood pressure and boosts immunity. Even simply smiling instead of frowning can do it, since the muscle movements correspond to mood-friendly chemicals in the brain.

The great journalist Norman Cousins suffered from terminal, crippling arthritis that doctors were sure would take his life far sooner than it did. Cousins created a program of healing for himself, one part of which was regular, daily laughter from watching old Marx Brothers movies. He'd stay in his house and watch movies that made him laugh, and it actually improved his health. He laughed, which triggered substances in his body that got rid of pain and ushered in healing. We can all be inspired by this story and learn to push through any pain by literally laughing it off.

So face your pain, remove your daggers and laugh at what you can't change. Pain (with laughter) is "The Gift."

Chapter 7
Energizology

"Energy: The capacity for work or vigorous activity; vigor; power."
– American Heritage Dictionary

The body is a vehicle that transports the mental, emotional and spiritual capacities inside of us. Like any vehicle, the body needs fuel to run properly.

What is body fuel? It's what we eat, both how much and how often. It's how we hydrate. It's how we exercise and move. And finally, it's how we sleep and rest.

Stress is energy expended; it *burns* our fuel. You actually have to do something to expend your energy, which can happen through your thoughts, your actions and your interactions with other people. We're always expending energy, no matter what we do. Even when we are sitting around or zoning out, we're using energy, because we're still thinking and breathing and feeling. Energy is not spent only in a physical sense. It's also spent mentally, emotionally and spiritually, and those are also the ways to replenish energy.

When we ruminate over a problem in our heads or listen to a person in crisis, we are expending *emotional* energy. We're putting our energy into trying to care and reason our way through a troubling

79

situation. We expend our *mental* energy when we do things like read this book, put together a report at work or help our kids with their homework. We spend our *spiritual* energy when we question our beliefs, about people, the meaning of life, or our values and ethics.

We're expending energy no matter what we do, so the biggest question is: are you refueling properly? Most people are not, from what I see in my work. Today, most of us are running at a frantic pace and end up overextending ourselves. We empty our energy reserves and then wonder *why the car won't run*.

How many times do you hear yourself or others say how stressed out they are or that they're waiting for life to calm down before they get healthy or start taking better care of themselves? In the meantime, they use *alternative* fuel replacements like caffeine, drugs or alcohol because they don't know how to cope correctly. But these alternative fuel replacements eventually are not enough.

Most people believe that sleep is the only way to build up our energy reserves, but, actually, we only get a portion of energy back from sleep (even a good night's sleep). In reality, we get energy from a variety of sources: food, hydration, sunlight, our belief system, our relationships, and, yes, sleep and rest. The bottom line is that we get energy from a lot of places. What differentiates it is the quality of energy we're getting. Is it good rest or bad rest? Good people or bad people? Healthy food or unhealthy food? The quality of our energy will make or break our performance.

We replenish our energy in the same ways we spend it. Food is *physical* fuel. Thoughts and imagination are *emotional* fuel. Rewarding work is *mental* fuel. A sense of purpose is *spiritual* fuel. All four capacities are interconnected and all forms of fuel can replenish all four areas of our life. Fuel usually has a way of getting to the proper depleted capacity that needs it most.

The foundation of living your best life and implementing everything you're reading about in this book comes from learning how to effectively and regularly fuel yourself. I call this *Energizology—* creating and maintaining a consistent level of energy so that we can pursue our plans for health, happiness and productivity.

FOOD IS FUEL

The easiest starting point for adequate body fuel is nutrition—what we eat, how much we eat and how often we eat. When we make choices about how to nourish ourselves with food and drink, the question is: how effective and efficient is that fuel we're putting in us? Caffeine is effective, but not efficient. It gives you a boost, temporarily, but it dehydrates the body and eventually you crash and need more caffeine. That's not a quality energy source. The millions of Americans who drink coffee to function are navigating on synthetic fuel, which is affecting their capacity to thrive.

The same fact applies to the food we eat. Food cravings are the result of the synthetic unhealthy foods, and/or emotional leakage affecting what we eat that doesn't properly nourish and recharge us. How many times are you hungry, and you grab something that's convenient instead of nourishing? Or you skip a meal to "make up" for that donut you splurged on earlier in the day? All that does is create a vicious cycle of not getting the fuel you need from food, which triggers more unhealthy cravings.

People tend to overeat not just when their physical reserves are out of whack, but also for emotional, spiritual and mental reasons. People often eat not because they're hungry, but because they're not getting the fuel they need in these other areas of their lives.

People will eat instead of getting the proper rest they need. Or they'll eat because they're not getting enough emotional or spiritual nourishment. Imagine feeling unsatisfied with yourself or your relationship or some other part of your life, but neglecting to fix it or find the meaning in it. Often, we eat to soothe the depletion we're feeling in other parts of our lives. Eating fulfills something you are not satisfied with, rather than fueling your physical requirements. You're eating to fill up two or three or four tanks, rather than just one tank! No wonder weight gain is the result— the body stores it as fat to keep you in survival mode.

The golden rule of eating for sustained energy is this: we must eat about every three hours consistently throughout the day in small portions. It can be something small, like a handful of nuts or some fruit, but if you don't eat every three hours, the body begins to lose energy. Blood sugar is regulated in three-hour modules. The food that we eat is transformed into energy by the body and it needs this type of fuel regularly.

When you eat one or two times a day, or even get your "three squares," your energy levels drop so far between meals that you've tripled the time the body takes to recalibrate.

Just like an athlete isn't going to eat a four-course meal before they go out on the field to play, we shouldn't expect to perform when we eat large quantities of food after hours of no food. It's a shock to the body.

The ideal routine is to eat 5-6 times a day: about 3 small meals with 2-3 snacks in between. A meal is defined as 500-700 calories and a snack is around

200 calories. Eating carbohydrates and protein together is ideal for staying fueled and full. Avoid sugary and fatty foods as much as possible. If you're craving a candy bar, have a piece of fruit, then a bit of candy afterwards if you're still craving it. As you start eating this way, you'll begin to notice you make fewer bad food choices because you aren't waiting until you're starving to eat.

Good hydration is the other key of consuming for optimal fuel. Most people are not properly hydrated, either because they drink soda (even diet), coffee and sugary juices instead of water, or they just can't be bothered to drink much of anything. You'll be amazed at the difference you see in your health if you start drinking more water than any other liquid during the day. Our body is 60% water. Most people don't realize how dehydrated they are until they start drinking enough water.

I believe in moderation. Every performer I've worked with—in sports, business or the military—uses this philosophy, and it works. I personally don't do well with diets and I don't really think diets work. Anything with the word "die" in it isn't good for me! We need to develop a way to eat to live, rather than to eat to deny ourselves.

Manufacturing and maintaining consistent, daily energy levels is the goal. Eating frequent, small meals is the first step towards that.

MOVEMENT IS FUEL

The second tenet of sustainable energy is regular physical activity. I know what you're thinking. *"Here we go again. Another book that's going to tell me I have to eat right and exercise to feel better."* But exercise doesn't have to be what most people think it does. It simply means we have *to move* on a regular basis.

My grandparents ate the best and worst food, but they lived long healthy lives because they got regular physical activity and fresh foods devoid of preservatives while living on a farm. Today, our corporate working world means that we sit at desks instead of harvesting crops, hauling machinery and working with our bodies. We also have every modern convenience to help us with our chores at home, which means no one is washing clothes in a bathtub and lugging coal up three flights of stairs for the stove. It's an easier life, we like to think, but we are so sedentary, we're gaining weight and experiencing health crises that threaten our lives.

While modern conveniences and work have changed, evolution has not. We still need regular physical activity. Our bodies were designed to be used throughout the lifespan. Any doctor will tell you that a muscle or physical capacity that's not used will eventually *atrophy*. The muscle will shrivel or the tissues will stiffen. Functioning will decline and injury can occur. We need to create the artificial conditions of health for our body, now that life no longer does. Every person needs 20-30 minutes of brisk physical activity at least 3-4 days a week. However, as I said, exercise gets a bad name. Physical activity doesn't mean you have to run or even jog. Neither does it mean you have to sweat profusely and turn red! What it does mean is you are walking briskly. You're not strolling. Think of walking when you're very late for something or when you're mildly concerned for your safety. That's what you need to do 3 or 4 days a week, for about a half hour. It doesn't have to be grueling, but you *do* have to move your body regularly.

People who say they want to give up or outsource all of their chores usually find they gain weight or lose performance. Chores like cleaning your house and carrying your groceries to and from the car are *good for you*! They keep your body conditioned and train various muscles that you may not even realize you're using. The next time you dread doing one of your chores, think of it as *giving* you energy, not taking away energy.

We also need movement when we're not exercising. Small changes in your daily life can help keep your body feeling alive. Take the stairs instead of the elevator. Walk up or down the escalator. Get up and walk around throughout the day if you sit at a desk.

Get off the bus one stop early. Do a few sets of sit-ups while you watch TV.

The bottom line? Use your body and it will continue serving you. Ignore it and you may discover how much you depend on it for daily performance.

REST AND SLEEP ARE FUEL

The third fundamental of creating and sustaining the body's energy reserves is proper rest. This one is so important that I've devoted an entire chapter to it, which follows next. In addition to sleeping well at night, we also need a quick splash of recovery *every 90-120 minutes* during our waking hours. This is the adult form of sleep that infants get throughout the day. As adults, we still need intervals of rest to function at our best. Sleep is *physical* and rest is *spiritual* and both fill up our energy tanks.

We'll talk all about the difference between sleep and rest in the next chapter and why it's biological, not decadent, to build a work-rest cycle into our day.

THE RULE OF 30 DAYS

You may think that all of this sounds like the typical health and exercise advice you've heard before and tried unsuccessfully to implement. However, the difference here, based on my experience of working with elite performers for the last decade, is that the plan I've just laid out isn't a gimmick. I'm not telling you to never eat dessert again or give up carbs. In fact, I think highly restrictive diets, like most fad nutrition movements, set people up for failure. Studies bear this out, too. Dieting doesn't work.

Ultimately, the people who lose weight and get healthy are the ones who make a *lifestyle* change. It's not just about looking better or fitting into a certain size (though that can certainly be a benefit!). Rather, it's about becoming your best self and respecting your body's needs to help get you there.

For people who've been on one diet or exercise regimen after another, it can seem insurmountable. You might begin to lose hope that anything will, in fact, work. I've found that if we can practice the same habit or routine consistently for 30 days, it becomes natural. That resistance to new habits begins to give way to effortless results, *if we stick with it for 30 days*. This applies to any kind of new learning. The autonomic nervous system literally imbeds the new habits into its programming and they start to become our new "automatic pilot." We can't fathom this at the time, because we're still running on our old habits, but we eventually see the rewards. Change takes discipline, and then you find that you have an easier time sticking to your routine.

In summary, we have to eat a certain way to energize our bodies. We have to hydrate and move our bodies. And we have to rest in 90-120 minute cycles and sleep proficiently throughout the night.

As you begin to make these habits a regular part of your routine, you'll find you're recharged and ready to go! You can *design* your life, versus life just *happening* to you. Energy is the fuel that drives us. Learning how to master your energy is "The Gift."

Chapter 8
Sleep vs. Rest

"Every now and then go away, have a little relaxation, for when you come back to your work your judgment will be surer."
– Leonardo DaVinci

If energy is the fuel we run on—the gasoline—then rest is the gas station where we fill our tanks back up.

I mentioned in the last chapter that *sleep is physical* and *rest is spiritual*. This distinction is a crucial one. Sleep is physical because it's something we need to recover a portion of our energy, as well as repair the wear-and-tear to the body that happens during the day. But we do not get all of our replenishment from the sleep cycle.

Rest is an equally necessary form of recovery. I call it our internal "peace-making process." Rest provides a needed respite in the midst of daily activity. Just as infants sleep and eat all throughout the day, we also need equal parts of rest and food throughout the day as adults. We don't need as much sleep, because we're not growing physically. But we still need regular periods of recovery to recharge us. That's why I say *rest is spiritual*. It nourishes us in an equally essential way as sleep does. Learning to incorporate rest *and* sleep into your life will make the difference you've been looking for in sustainable energy.

Neglecting our need for regular periods of rest throughout the day is another example of how we work against our basic wiring (like only eating 2-3 times a day). Part of what's so vital about rest is the role it plays in our ability to recover from the daily stress of life. As I've said before, stress isn't the problem, but rather our *response* to that stress and how quickly we recover. Lack of recovery is the main reason so many of us have trouble coping with the demands of today's fast-paced world. Society has programmed us to believe that more and faster are always better, but that is not true.

Corporate America in particular has been slow to catch on to this fact. The motto is *work, work and work more*; however, the most consistently productive people are the ones who learn how to keep refueling their engines throughout the day, through proper eating, hydrating, exercise and *rest cycles*. Rest gets a bad rap among people who think it's lazy or an ineffective use of their time.

In reality, rest is natural and productive. When you take care of yourself, you probably notice you respond better to stress. When you're pushing yourself in one or more areas of your life, your response to stress takes more out of you.

How fast is your speed of recovery? Think about the four cylinders you run on: the mental, emotional, spiritual and physical. Mentally, when you get distracted, how long does it take you to get back to what you were doing? Emotionally, when you're angry or upset, how quickly can you get back to a neutral or even a happy state? Spiritually, how soon can you get back in touch with your belief system and your core self when it's challenged? Physically, how quickly can you recover after you've lost energy? And in all of these cases, how healthy is that recovery strategy? Smoking a cigarette may help you recover quickly from a moment of stress, but it's not healthy.

Infants and toddlers recover almost immediately from stress, because they *know how to recover*. They don't know any different! They sleep or they zone out or they ask for something to eat. Ultimately, by tuning back into your natural rhythms—many of which you learned about in the last chapter—you're going to respond to stress much more effectively. Rest is the final tool in that arsenal.

Acknowledging our need to recover helps us get back in touch with our natural rhythms, which propel us forward in our day and in life. You're going to be more productive and create more positive momentum by *resting* properly. Stress will always be there, so by recovering regularly, you are arming yourself to win the battle against something that is never going to change!

REST IS SPIRITUAL

Studies show that 90 minutes is the optimal peak performance window; two hours is the maximum. Sports games follow this natural law. Football, basketball, hockey and baseball are punctuated by periodic breaks: time-outs, quarters and halftimes. The athletes recover, so they can refuel and keep on playing. Without such periods of rest, even the best players would stop performing.

We're the same, even if we're not running down a basketball court or rounding the bases. It doesn't matter what we're doing, whether we are working or playing, active or inactive. Without recovery, our mental, emotional, spiritual and physical acuities drop dramatically after two hours. We need brief, periodic breaks to restore our sharpness.

In other words, we need a mini-vacation every 90-120 minutes! What exactly does that mean? It means a minimum of a 2-5 minute break. We should push the envelope and work as hard as we can for 90-120 minutes, take a break and do it again. Eventually, your day will look like a wavy line of activity and recovery, activity and recovery, in regular 90-120 minute cycles. In fact, I lay out my day in 90-minute segments and find it's so much easier and productive to deal with what the day holds in intervals.

STRESS RECOVERY

A manual for the victims, volunteers and heroes of Hurricane Season 2005.

by

Terry Lyles, Ph.D.

www.terrylyles.com

Your 2-5 minute break can be anything: surf online, meditate, go outside, put your head down, get a drink of water or listen to some music. Anything that breaks one cycle of activity and prepares you for the next. That break will re-infuse you mentally, emotionally and physically, *if* you have the right recovery strategy. It's different for everyone and you may have to play around with it to figure out what's right for you. The key is taking these breaks regularly.

People who have learned to listen to their body, to read its signals and respond accordingly discover that they have more energy over a longer period of time, and consistently perform at a higher level of *efficiency* and *excellence*. Most people usually do not figure this out because they have become programmed by society's mantra that says, "*Keep working. More is better. The longer you work, the better person you are.*"

That's crazy. It's like trying to hold your hand over your head for an hour. You can't do it. Eventually, the blood rushes out of it, gravity takes over and it drops. Every day we have to fight the "gravity" of bad programming in our lives, our work and our families. We need rest, about every 90-120 minutes to be exact!

SLEEP IS PHYSICAL

Sleep is another habit we need to regulate for the best possible performance. In addition to neglecting our need for periodic rest throughout the day, most Americans do not get enough sleep. Sleep regulates every aspect of our being—mood, immune function, memory, metabolism and virtually every other process imaginable. As a result, sleep deprivation hinders our ability to respond to stress effectively and live our best life. Many people become so accustomed to poor sleeping habits that they don't realize sleep deprivation is causing them difficulties in multiple areas of life.

Sleep is another component of that basic *wiring*. It's important that we learn to work with it, rather than against it. We need to power down from the activity of the day before we go to bed, just like a computer does. People tend to think their sleep problems are the result of psychological problems or stress, and they might be. But more often than you might expect, it's the simple things we do before we go to sleep that set us up for unrestful sleep! A good sleep routine can resolve many seemingly chronic sleep problems.

Because of the body's natural rhythms, it responds well to sleep routines. The more routine we can build into our sleep pattern, the better. Here are some tips:

- Go to bed at the same time every night and wake up at the same time every morning. Your body will rapidly adjust to this routine, and you'll find it's easier to fall asleep and wake up.

- Limit stimuli about a half-hour before bedtime. This means no television (especially the evening news, which is highly anxiety-provoking), avoid deep conversations at home or on the telephone, no difficult reading and no strenuous physical activity. If you like to read, limit it to something light and enjoyable that will help you relax and unwind.

- Don't eat 90 minutes before bedtime, since your digestion will interfere with falling and/or staying asleep. Avoid caffeine after lunchtime, if you think it might be interfering with your sleep. Studies have found that caffeine can take up to eight hours to metabolize. Sleep, not coffee or soda, should be fueling you.

- Sleep in a dark, cool room. Eliminate light as much as possible, whether outside or inside. Invest in room-darkening shades if you get up after dawn.

- If you wake up in the middle of the night, don't look at the clock! *Learning the time will only put your brain into analytical mode and trigger anxiety, making it less likely to ascertain quality rest. Don't do it!*

- Don't hit the snooze button. Get up, turn on the lights and start your day.

YOU *CAN* BE WELL-RESTED

I hear many people say that they simply can't be well rested, because life is too hectic. Their kids keep them awake. Or they have to clean the house at night. Or they'll lose their job if they don't take work home. That's the "real world." It's almost become a badge of honor to be sleep-deprived, as if it means you are busy and productive. However, it's just another example of bad programming and *giving into* stress, instead of taking responsibility for ourselves and saying *no*.

I really started to recognize the difference between sleep and rest with my son, Brandon. I basically didn't sleep well for 20 years, because of alternating shifts throughout the night, every night. I had to learn how to *rest* to live and to survive.

I learned to rest by maximizing my quiet time, through meditation and prayer; exercising, which I've always loved; and good eating habits. In the early years of Brandon's illness, I had lots of reading to do while I was completing my doctorate program. During my shifts at night, I would literally stand up against the wall and read while Brandon was sleeping, both to keep me awake and to stay on top of my studies.

During the day, I was taking those much-needed rest cycles to refresh myself, since I couldn't sleep much. That's why I know the power of regular rest cycles during the day—I did it for twenty years! I haven't died because of my chronic lack of sleep, and I'm actually blessed to be in great shape and health for my age. In fact, not only did I survive that process with Brandon, I learned to *thrive* in it. I tried to beat it as much as possible by doing the right things while I was awake.

This lends itself to another important distinction about rest: it's not an excuse to start copping-out of your responsibilities. Throwing away your to-do list or giving in to the fact that you are never going to have your life in order is *not* the proper application of rest. It's an excuse. Real rest happens when you are productive and taking care of your to-dos, while getting regular breaks.

Loose ends in your life are more of an energy drain than doing the tasks themselves. The time you spend in the thought process, thinking about them and avoiding them, burns through energy. Unfinished business drains your capacity. Just do it and it's out of your psyche.

REST IS THE GIFT

I've quoted the Bible several places in this book and I want to make a brief point. When I quote the Bible,

I'm not promoting any specific religion. I'm offering the passages as wisdom, like any great text and like the great people I've quoted at the beginning of each chapter. Spirituality is a personal thing for everyone. In my case, my study of theology rounded out my understanding of the blueprint of human nature. I find it's an unusual mix because most people don't believe in both "schools." I believe that spirituality provides the missing link among psychology and physiology. Rarely are these differing schools of thought put together like this, and there is wisdom in it.

The concept of rest shows up in the Bible 305 times. In Matthew 11:28, Jesus says: "Come to me, all you who are weary and burdened, and I will give you rest." He doesn't say I'll give you sleep, because you can't give someone sleep. But you can give someone rest by helping them understand the importance of letting something go spiritually and emotionally.

You can offer a shoulder to cry on or a helping hand and relieve another person's burdens. You can give them the formula for rest. *We don't have to sleep to get rest*, which is why those pit stops during the day are so important. As adults, we need to honor our wiring, and get the mental, emotional, spiritual *and* physical rest we need. All of us need that quick 2-5 minutes of rest every 90-120 minutes to recharge our batteries. It's vitally important that we understand the difference between sleep and rest.

The energy needed to recharge our system every day is abundantly available. If we continue running ourselves on an energy deficit, we will find ourselves wearing down and running out. Developing an "abundance" mentality about our ability to recharge, and putting routines that honor our natural rhythms into practice, will transform the way we live. Each of us has abundant resources of energy for working hard, playing hard and enjoying life to the fullest *every day*. Once we learn how to tap into our energy sources, we'll realize we have all the energy we need to meet the regular demands of the day, and the extraordinary demands of life.

By respecting our stress and recovery cycles and moving between them throughout the day, we build and sustain our physiological and psychological momentum, which leads to peak performance and productivity. We need balanced work-rest cycles to secure the health, happiness and productivity we seek.

Rest is a basic need, and if honored, will change your life. Rest is "The Gift."

Chapter 9
Emotion Is the Breath of Life

*"The emotions aren't always immediately subject to reason,
but they are always immediately subject to action."*
– William James

The word "emotion" literally means "to set in motion." Our emotions are the gauges that propel us forward and tell us we are alive. Anything that stimulates our senses triggers an emotional response. Our biggest challenge is learning to interpret those responses and navigate our way through them.

Emotions can feel overwhelming. Many of us try to deal with our emotions by ignoring them or giving into them. We allow our emotions to control us. However, emotion is nothing more than mind-body language— it's a dialect that's going on between the mind and the body. Emotions are not logical. We may feel a certain way and not know where that emotion is coming from, and then it ends up affecting our life in ways it shouldn't.

We're trained from very young not to let our emotions "run us." When I was in high school, I had a knee injury that would periodically flare up. One day, I told my mom I couldn't mow the lawn that week, because I wasn't feeling great. My mom responded, "*If feeling was a criteria for performing, I would be dead,*" explaining that there were many times she hadn't felt like waking up in the middle of the night to feed me or to run after me when I was little, but she did it anyway. Well, I mowed the lawn that same day and I ended up learning an important lesson: *emotion is not a criterion for performance*. Some days we just have to suck it up and do what's required of us.

However, a relationship between emotion and performance does exist. If you take emotion completely out of your relationships and your day, you end up with a plastic life. You're just going through the motions when you *disconnect* from your emotions. The key is to manage your emotions.

How many of you feel like you're living this way? Have you zoned out and you're going through the motions to keep going? Corporate America, in particular, has taken the emotion out of everything, to the point that people don't know why they're doing something and they don't feel good about it. Many of us attempt to *turn off* our emotion for 40 or more hours a week, like a tourniquet, and we suffer the consequences at work and at home. The emotion *always* leaks out in other ways.

We also navigate our relationships with emotional tourniquets. Many people are just getting by instead of listening to the *emotions* they're having about their relationships. As I've said, it's easier to keep things the way they are, even when they're not great, than it is to change. Many people think any "bad" emotions about their partner or their relationship are too scary to deal with and it takes a crisis to finally force them to confront these emotions.

Whether at work or in our relationships, we need to allow the natural dialogue of emotion to flow inside of us. It's entirely normal to feel different and even extreme emotions. We can move very quickly from one mood to another. It's not so much *what* you feel, but *how long* you stay in that place. How long are you angry? How long are you fearful? How long are you depressed? Our outlook and approach in life gets skewed when we stay in negative emotional states for too long.

Recovery speed is vital where our emotions are concerned.

THE EMOTIONAL FUELS THE PHYSICAL, MENTAL AND SPIRITUAL

Prolonged negative emotional states are harmful to your health in all ways. Negative emotion triggers the release of cortisol, the body's stress hormone. While it's a great chemical to mobilize us when we're in a situation of danger—activating that "fight or flight" mechanism in the body—over time, cortisol wreaks havoc on body and mind. Too much cortisol fries the immune system and traps us in a vicious cycle of declining mental, emotional, spiritual and physical health. Studies show that women, in particular, are prone to the damaging effects of cortisol, especially when it's the result of a troubled marriage or other troubled relationships.

There is a clear link between our emotional state and our physical health. Whether you're frustrated at work or unhappy with your relationship, you vote yourself out of your best life simply by settling for high levels of negative emotion.

In addition to knowing when it's time to make a life change personally or professionally, we must learn to recognize negative emotion and transition out of it quickly. It comes down to knowing *yourself*. We're all predisposed to certain emotional states because of our individual wiring. Some people may be prone to ADHD, others to depression, but *we can modify it*. We have more control over our thoughts and emotions than we believe we do. We can't control what pops up in our mind, but we can control how long we focus on a certain thought or emotion.

Depression can be defined as *looking at the wrong thing for too long*. Before you know it, you begin to breathe, act and expect in a depressed way. It's very important that we understand what's in our power to change: it's our perception. Ninety percent of reality is perception and ten percent is unchangeable. We have to identify that 10%—other people's behavior, taxes, the weather—all of the things that aren't going to change, and then spend our time and energy focusing on the other 90%.

Otherwise, we end up acting out with compensatory behavior: we drink or smoke too much, we gossip about other people, we get depressed, we watch too much TV, or a million other diversions, all because we're not dealing with our emotions in a proactive way.

We have options when dealing with how we feel, but the first key is *knowing that*. We have to be in control of what we think about, inside and outside of us—our wiring and the world around us. Sound emotional health asks that you come to the realization that: *I can control what I think, what I feel, what I believe and what I do. The rest is out of my control.*

YOU'RE AN ATHLETE IN LIFE

I made the connection between emotion and quick recovery because of my training in sports science.

My background was in psychology, but as I went through many years of training hundreds of patients and families, there always was a gap that didn't fit for me. It wasn't until after I finished my degree and started doing sports science and training that the light bulb went off for me. It literally changed how I train people to increase personal health, happiness, and productivity.

I learned that in sports, you can't stop and take a breather to *feel better* when you're in the midst of performance and chaos. My mission became figuring out how to help someone achieve emotional recovery in a moment of stress, pro-athlete or not.

Every emotion has a toxicity value. When we feel a toxic emotion, like anger, it doesn't fuel us efficiently. That negative emotion is a drain on our performance. Like the fuel we talked about in earlier chapters, all emotions have a certain "octane." The emotion is filling us up and the question is: How well does it *fuel* us?

We need to take a training mentality towards our life and learn to master our emotions so we fuel ourselves in a way that helps us, not hinders us. All it takes is 30 seconds to do it!

CHANGE YOUR BREATH, CHANGE YOUR LIFE

Our emotions and our breath are interconnected on a physiological level. Oxygen fuels the blood and that fuel comes from our breath, which is different depending on how we're feeling in that moment.

All emotions have a "breath-print." One way to identify your emotions is to identify your breath. This is helpful because, often, we don't know what we're feeling. Likewise, if you want to change your emotional state, you change your breathing state. How simple is that?

An emotional navigram from sport science will help to illustrate how emotions relate to each other and how we can navigate our emotional states. The navigram classifies emotions according to energy levels and whether the emotion is positive or negative. An emotion can generate a lot of energy or a little energy, regardless of whether it is a good or a bad emotion.

The two quadrants on the right house positive emotions and the two on the left house negative emotions. The upper-right quadrant contains positive emotions with a *high-energy* output, like excitement and feeling "pumped." Below it is the quadrant of positive emotions with a *low-energy* output, like calmness and relaxation. I've done the same with negative emotions. High-energy negative emotions like anger and fear, and low-energy negative energy emotions like sadness and boredom.

Navigram Awareness

Inspiration

Anger Fear Frustration Anxiety	Excited Connected Challenged Pumped
Sad Depressed Lonely Exhausted	Calm Peaceful Relaxed Recharged

θ E•mot•ions $\oplus$

Performance is measured in the speed of recovery.

We are always moving between quadrants, or different emotional states. But while circumstances or people may trigger certain emotions, how we navigate them makes all the difference. Choosing between sadness, depression, excitement, calmness and joy is *up to us*.

So how can we move from a negative emotional state to a positive emotional state quickly and independent of our circumstances? We breathe.

As I mentioned, each quadrant of emotion is associated with a specific pattern of breathing, or "breath-print." Whatever quadrant we are in emotionally, we breathe according to the breath-print of that quadrant; it is natural and it is physiological. This fact allows us both to recognize the emotional "zone" we are in *and* get out of it.

Quadrant	Breath Print
High Positive	*Fast, deep breath in* through the nose and a *fast breath out* through the mouth.
Low Positive	*Deep, slow breath in* through the nose, and a *slow breath out* through the mouth. It is a relaxing, calming breath. For the most relaxing breath, make your exhale twice as long as the inhale.
Low Negative	*Shallow breath in* and a *slow breath out* through the mouth… the breath of a sigh.
High Negative	*Shallow breath in* through the mouth and a *fast breath out* through the mouth…the beginning of hyperventilation. This is the fight or flight breath.

Practicing the breath of a positive quadrant allows you to transition out of a negative emotion, within seconds. Let's say you have a bad morning, but you have to go to a meeting and be positive and upbeat. Or, the reverse. You have a rough day at work and you have to go home to your children or you have a date with your partner that night. The simple exercise of breathing can enable you to respond the way you *want to*.

Or how about when your mother says something frustrating or hurtful to you? Or your partner does something you feel is inconsiderate? Or your child tests your patience?

Breathe!

If you are in the *high negative* quadrant—feeling angry or fearful—and want to move to the positive side, the quickest way is to take two or three *high positive* breaths: deep in through the nose and fast out through the mouth. This transports enough oxygen into the blood so your system interprets that you are moving in that direction physiologically. Your emotions *have* to follow because emotions and breath are interconnected. One goes where the other goes, so why not lead with your breath?

Take care to ensure you are breathing in through the *nose*. Most people mouth-breathe out of the top of the lungs, shallowly. When you breathe in through the mouth, the oxygen is not filtered and it stalls in the top part of the lungs, instead of reaching the lower part of the lungs where it transfers more quickly to the rest of the body. Deep belly-breathing through the nose is better because it is first filtered and it gets the oxygen into the body faster and more thoroughly (this is the breath of yoga).

EMOTION IS THE BREATH OF LIFE

Emotions and energy are interconnected. In fact, they are inseparable. *Remember the word "emotion" literally means movement!* Working with your emotions is a key part of achieving your best life. How many people have a goal to be on anti-depressants this year? Or to be exhausted all the time? Many people end up in poor emotional states because they don't have a *plan* not to go there.

What goes up must come down. It's gravity. No one can stay in negative emotional states forever. Eventually, you will be forced down by gravity to recover. The question is whether this recovery will be voluntary or involuntary. Will you be proactive in choosing to face your challenges and problems, or will you wait until gravity slams you into involuntary action? One is a voluntary choice and the other is a reflex that nobody plans on experiencing.

In addition to eating and hydrating properly, getting the right balance of rest and activity, and *breathing* through our tough emotional times, we take our life in the direction *we want it to go*.

Our best life requires a clear understanding of our emotional make-up, as well as the connection that exists between our emotions, our speed of recovery and our breath. If we can control our breath, we can

113

control the energy flow in our body and we control our emotions!

Learning to control your emotions instead of allowing them to control you is "The Gift."

Chapter 10
What's Your Purpose?

"First say to yourself what you would be; and then do what you have to do."
– Epictetus

I want to focus on the process of understanding how our lives *mean* something. And how that meaning, if we extract it correctly, produces a future for us that will leave behind a satisfying legacy.

I call this *life purpose*—the reason we're here on this planet. Life purpose relates to the spiritual part of our being. We move beyond the mechanics of life, the *how* of life, to touch on the *why* of life. The *how* of life has a tangible answer. We eat, we sleep, we work and so on. The *why*, or purpose of our life, is less tangible. It's what separates us from plants and rocks and other animals. We have a belief system and free will, and it's full of many different flavors and variations. Passion, motivation, perseverance and force all flow from the *why* of life.

You can't live your life without an understanding of your purpose, and you can't understand your purpose without going through a process of spirituality.

Many people shy away from the discussion of spirituality because it's too personal, but I believe we have to talk about it. Spirituality links our emotional, mental and physical capacities. What you believe about your purpose in life influences how you think, feel and act. Connecting to your life purpose is always a spiritual undertaking, though it may look different for each person. Purpose is not about religion, though the two may coincide for some people.

Ultimately, life doesn't discriminate. Whether you're a Buddhist, a Christian or an atheist, you still have to ask yourself the same questions to tap into your purpose. What is the purpose of my existence? Why am I here? How do I connect with that on a regular basis?

It sounds heavy, but questioning our existence this way repositions us and prompts us to pause and ask the other important questions. Why am I doing this job? What do I really like to do? Who do I love? Why does that excite me? Why does this infuriate me? An examination of our life's purpose keeps us real and on the ground, while still looking around at the wonder and beauty of our world.

So often we fly through life without thinking about the big picture. We live from minute to minute and day to day and week to week with no clear end in mind. We have no plan of action and, therefore, don't think through the meaning and consequences of our actions. This causes us to make bad decisions or end up somewhere we never wanted to be.

A fulfilled life is a life lived *with the big picture always in view*. Think of navigating your life like an airplane. The radar screen will show you where you are and what is all around you. Each of us must determine for ourselves why we are here and where we are going. That is why identifying and knowing our personal belief system is so important. It is literally our *map* in life.

Figuring out the *why* of your life is like looking out of that airplane from 20,000 feet up: Who are you? Where are you? What's next? We need that perspective to clearly define what is most important to us. Life purpose is shaped and defined by the beliefs you hold so strongly that you are willing to stake your life on them. Your true purpose animates your spirit, and creates meaning and fulfillment in everything you do.

Elite performers know how to find this *purpose zone*— the mind-body connection that we call spirituality or life purpose—and when you can engage in life on that level on a regular basis, it's very powerful *and* productive.

Your life's purpose is essentially your reason for living and the overriding inspiration for all your actions. Life purpose is not something you arrive at, but something that you live by each day. Everyone has a purpose. The task is to figure out yours.

MOTIVATION VS. INSPIRATION

Each year, most people make at least one New Year's resolution, whether it's starting a new diet, quitting smoking, going to church or any number of countless other self-improvement endeavors. However, by February 1st, most people are right back to where they started just four weeks earlier—living the way they were before the resolution. They just can't sustain it.

Why? Because their *motivation* wears off—it's gravity. When you make a resolution, it's an external stimuli trying to work internal change. Motivation is fleeting because it comes from outside of us, rather than inside of us.

Motivation is actually a secondary response to something much more powerful and fundamental: *inspiration.*

The Hebrew word "neshamah" can be translated into English as "inspire" or "breath." So to inspire means to breathe life, into yourself, the world and others. The difference between motivation and inspiration is that inspiration is *internal*. It comes from inside. Inspiration is the lifeblood that keeps us going and focused on the *big picture*. It's the fuel that sustains us, so we continue living our life as we're meant to. Inspiration derives from an inner source that is constantly renewing itself.

Motivation, on the other hand, is not anchored deep inside of us and, therefore, we can't sustain it. Motivation is what's at work when we see a thin, attractive person and decide we want to be thin and attractive, so we go on a diet. It's what's at work when we say we want to be rich, so we get the highest power job we think will get us there the fastest. Eventually, we're going to lose the willpower or the passion to pursue these goals, because they are not connected to our core belief system.

Instead, we must find what we are aligned with deep inside: our inspiration. A lack of motivation or passion for the life you are living or the inability to achieve your goals is merely a symptom. The root of the problem is a *lack of purpose*. Align yourself with your purpose, and passion, motivation and the rest of it will flow forth as by-products, naturally.

Exceptional people in every area of life have learned the difference between inspiration and motivation at some level even though they may not explain it this way. They know that internal power (inspiration) is the energetic force that gets them up early in the morning and keeps them up late enjoying life to the fullest.

The power for lasting change comes from knowing what drives you. The question is: *what does this mean for you?* Only *you* can figure it out. It's different for everybody, but you really have to tune into that drive so that you can use it to propel yourself forward in the direction you want to go.

Motivation relates to what we *do*; inspiration relates to who we *are*. If you can identify what inspires you, it will change not just what you do, but *who you are*.

PURPOSE ALIGNMENT

For many years, it was a mystery to me how good people with solid values could make foolish and unhealthy decisions. But it happens all the time. A person who is good at their core somehow goes off track. Bad decisions, bad jobs or bad relationships take life in a different direction than they would have intended.

When we function as we're meant to, our *values* shape our *life purpose,* and the way we live out our *life purpose* reflects our *values*. So what goes wrong when we make decisions that run counter to our values and our life purpose? Usually, it means a disconnect has occurred in the alignment of our purpose and our values. For whatever reason, we don't relate *what we do* to *what we believe*.

Of course, we're only human. We aren't perfect specimens who are never going to feel lazy or give into temptation or think we can get away with something. We have free will, which means we can *choose* to do something, even when we know it's wrong or runs counter to our values. It's flipside of what separates us from other life forms—not only can we choose to make our life full of purpose, we also can choose not to.

However, when it happens repeatedly and you end up at, *"How did I get here?"* a more fundamental process is at work. To a large degree, the tension between our values and our purpose comes down to brain function. While the left hemisphere of the brain deals with logic, time, and the processing and storage of information, the right hemisphere of the brain has a very different function. The right brain has no sense of logic or time, instead it processes things like our visual-spatial perception, music and emotions.

Ultimately, our values are a *left-brain* function and our life purpose is a *right-brain* function. Values have to do with knowledge and information, while purpose deals with vision. A critical part of aligning the two and getting the two sides to work together, rather than separately, is identifying our life purpose and living it in everything we do.

This *purpose alignment* helps us mesh together our right- and left-brain functions into a coordinated flow. We link our values and behavior with our purpose.

WHAT'S YOUR PURPOSE?

When I was working with tsunami victims in Thailand, I met hundreds of people who had no home, no income and little hope for a full recovery of their former lives. Many of them were working tirelessly to rebuild what had once been home, but now resembled a war zone. My compassion overflowed for the thousands of people whose lives would never be the same. A natural disaster that lasted only minutes would affect the land and these people for a lifetime.

Over the course of about three weeks, with the help of a Thai interpreter, I counseled many family and international forensic medical teams and rescue workers on stress and recovery. My job was to restore hope and guide these people, as much as I could, along a path that would provide a new inspiration for living. I tried to provide them with the skills to renew their hope and energy towards a recovery process of health, inspiration and a new future.

All of us are on a similar journey. Ultimately, life is a cycle, no matter who we are. We're born, we die and we do something in the middle—we live! It's about what we do during that process of living that makes a difference. Some people are just getting by because they haven't discovered *their life* and what makes them feel alive. Ultimately, it comes down to feeling connected, to yourself, to others and to the world, and believing that your life makes a difference and fits into the grand scheme of things, however you envision that.

Figuring out *your life* is so important, because each day is too precious to waste and, once gone, will never come back. Each of us can be *anything we want to be*. We merely have to feel our purpose, and then, one step at a time, live it. Living life to the fullest means being connected to *your* life purpose, and no one but you can figure it out. Once triggered, your life purpose will release the passion, motivation, perseverance and success you've been waiting for. Purpose is "The Gift."

Chapter 11
Hope Is the Canvas of Life

"Hope is the dream of a soul awake."
– French proverb

Hope is the canvas of life. We paint the details of our goals, aspirations and dreams onto the canvas of hope, but they're merely the colors and the brushstrokes. Without hope, we have nothing to paint on.

The word "hope" has its roots in Old English and German, which give the word a base meaning of "trust." There is a great distinction here. While we tend to view hope as a gamble or, in worse states of mind, an empty waste of our time, the original word suggests none of that uncertainty. Hope is the equivalent of trust, which is the confident expectation of something or someone. When you trust, you rely on the integrity, ability or character of a person or thing. You trust that everything will be as it should be. Hope is not a pie-in-the-sky endeavor. Rather, it's the way to create what we want and need.

Some dictionaries also suggest that hope is connected to the word "hop," as in taking a leap. When you hope, you take a leap in expectation. *Hope is the ultimate exercise in visualization.*

Hope is also the foundation of any healing process, whether mental, emotional, spiritual or physical. This is especially true of people with physical diseases. The medical establishment will tell you that attitude is a huge part of healing. A person's expectations—in other words, their hope—powerfully shape how their body responds to disease. People spontaneously heal. Couples who struggle with infertility for years suddenly have a baby. Studies find that "the placebo effect" is alive and well—people who are given inactive sugar pills for comparison purposes often experience an improvement in symptoms, an improvement in physical or emotional health *with no medical intervention*. They *believe* they are getting better, so they do.

Likewise, people who give into illness often find that their expectations are met. Studies show that individuals who are optimistic, even in the face of fatal diagnoses, live longer lives or in some cases heal. Magic Johnson has been living with HIV since 1991. He's a living example of mind over matter coupled with good medical treatment (and also happens to be an elite athlete who has likely mastered his response to stress).

Too often, physical illness or not, people simply give up, give into life and settle. They never give themselves the opportunity to reach their full potential or heal from past wounds, whether physical, mental, emotional or spiritual. They think life has no further fruits to bear. Or, it hurts too much to hope for anything better after so much disappointment in the past. But without hope, a person doesn't have much in life.

HOPE GROWS

A great inspiration for hope is to think of children. They look at everything with hope, because they have a whole future ahead of them! They dream big about what and who they're going to be when they grow up. They look forward to each day because it's full of new discovery. As we grow up, we often think we should have arrived at our destination. Yet adulthood is not a place you arrive at; abandoning "childish" hopes and dreams is actually counterproductive. In fact, as we do *grow up* and grow older, it's essential to continue chasing after our hopes and dreams as we did when we were young. We *grow up* and forget our basic wiring. We respond to bad programming that tells us to neglect our dreams and desires because we're adults now. It's essential, whether you're 9 or 90, to have hopes and aspirations, even if you've achieved great things in your lifetime. Otherwise, you begin to flounder and settle in.

Just as children need things in front of them to keep them occupied (remember my mother's saying about an empty mind being the devil's workshop?), so too do adults need purpose and learning in their lives.

The "toys" may change, but the same dynamic remains. We need to be solidly anchored to a sense of purpose and hope; otherwise we risk falling away from the true course our life should take. We take ourselves out of the game of life by giving up on hope.

People without hope make themselves miserable and ill, and do the same to those around them. When people start nosing into other people's business, it's because they don't have their own canvas—their own hope and life. I see this a lot in older people. When someone is obsessed with illness or what everyone else is doing, I tell them they *need to get a life*! Too much gossip or involvement in other people's business is a sign that we're not investing enough in our own life. We all need to have our own stuff going on.

The good news is that someone else can come along and give us hope. They can lend us their canvas to paint on, until we find our own. We can give people hope and we can take hope from someone! It's all about refusing to give up on hope—*no matter what*. Life throws us obstacles and challenges, and it's up to us to hang onto our hope, since it's the foundation for getting us through those times.

I learned that I couldn't let life squash my hope when doctors told my wife and me that our son, Brandon, wouldn't live through childhood, then adolescence. Twenty-one years later, he's still here. I just never gave up. I never allowed anyone to take away our hope. Brandon's NOS diagnosis made it challenging to believe we could care for and help him, because the medical field made it seem hopeless. There was no diagnosis and no answers. And even though we couldn't find answers, I had to believe *against* that negative hope each day and live my life. I also saw in Brandon such a tenacity to live. I learned so much from him.

Sometimes people give up and say they have no other choice. They throw their hands up and give in. But there's *always* a choice. It's an easy cop-out to say a tragedy or a disease will rule your life, when really we're standing in the midst of so much potential discovery and greatness. Hope is what allows us to unearth it.

PLANTING THE SEEDS OF HOPE

Hope, like many great qualities, is sown in childhood. Proverbs 22:6 says: "Train up a child in the way he should go; and when he is old, he will not depart from it."

The phrase "train up" literally means to restrict but not choke. The word picture here is a stake that you would use to bolster a tomato plant to allow it to grow. When a tomato plant starts growing, it's just leaves and stalk. When the fruit begins to grow, it's too heavy and, without support, it will fall onto the ground and rot. The purpose of the stake is to support the fruit and prevent it from falling to the ground, so it can mature and thrive.

The stake is a metaphor for the gentle structure children require to grow up with hope, among other characteristics. The goal in raising a child is to provide the support they need to thrive. Parenting can either destroy hope or feed it. As I discussed before, too much or too little discipline will destroy hope. It's a delicate balance, just like staking the tomato plant.

Ideally, what we're trying to do in parenting is train a child upward. This implies that when we are born, we're already falling downward. We don't train children to do bad; it's already in the DNA. We train them to do right and do good, which is part of the discipline process. However, if you do it too harshly or without explanation, it destroys the child's hope. Likewise, if you let your child run wild without the supportive structure of discipline, he or she will fail to thrive. A child who doesn't have hope often ends up in alternative lifestyles, like drugs or teenage pregnancy.

So many children today are growing up without hope because parenting is a 24/7 job that requires significant discipline on the part of the parent, as well. Most people have no idea about the kind of challenge they're signing up for when they have a child. Many wonder, "*What was I thinking?*" But as parents, we owe it to ourselves and our children to make the best of it and do the right thing. We're called upon to give our children a solid foundation for life, and hope is that foundation, tenderly cultivated with consistent and proper discipline.

As we watch children grow and develop around us, it's important to realize that it's never too late to start mentoring someone. A mentor is basically a person who walks along beside you, who has more life experience than you and is willing to take you by the arm and walk with you through the storms. It takes a lot of patience and time, but the payoff is priceless. The parenting process is where hope is made or broken, but fortunately, other people can come to our aid.

GROW YOUR OWN HOPE

People who didn't get the hope they needed growing up should realize they can still have someone come into their life, at any point, who can be a mentor. And, perhaps more importantly, *they* can be a mentor to sow the seeds of hope within themselves. One of best ways to become encouraged is to encourage others. Get out of yourself. If you don't think your life has meaning or hope, serve somebody else and you'll produce hope in yourself, even though it wasn't bred in you. Visit the elderly, volunteer, read books to kids—just do something and you'll find it comes back to you.

We're all born with a measure of faith, in ourselves and life. It's in there. The issue is *will that faith be lived out in our life?* Or will it be squelched by fear, anger and anxiety? If your parents didn't build hope, you can build it in yourself.

Look at Oprah, who came from a broken background and now builds hope every day for millions and millions of people. I give to people because I get more out of it than they do. You can never "out-give" because you're going to get rewards back in more ways than you give! That shouldn't be the goal, but *you're going to harvest what you plant, time after time*. It's gravity. If I plant an apple seed, I'll get an apple tree. Likewise, if I'm constantly tearing people down, belittling them and criticizing them, I'm planting a weed. You can't hope for a harvest from a bad seed. There are so many critical lessons we learn from the nurturing process, and it's easier to do it right from as early as possible in life, but it's never too late to begin sowing good seed.

When my son, Brent, was five or six years old, the movie *Batman* was coming out and all he wanted for Christmas was a Batmobile. They were hard to find because the movie was not even in theaters yet, but I found one and I brought it home and showed it to him. Brent was so excited! I asked him, *"How many little boys like you do you think will never get a toy like this for Christmas or ever?"* I told him that nothing is truly his, including the toy. I was giving it to him, just as I gave him his other toys, his house and even his brother! Brent couldn't conceive of this at the time, like any child his age. I was really trying to teach him the lesson that it's not just about you; it's about "we."

I told Brent that we're going to drive to inner city Detroit and give the Batmobile away to a boy. Brent of course begged me not to do it, but we did. We went to Detroit and gave the Batmobile to a little boy, who, along with his mom, was so amazed he didn't think we were for real! Brent thought the Batmobile was gone forever. But, lo and behold, on Christmas morning he opened his presents and he found another one. He thought it was the greatest thing that had ever happened to him! And he learned that what you give away, you always get back.

Just a few years later, Brent was on mission trips, giving of himself to others in need. He had already become a great person, who cares about people and gives to people. He was raised up to believe in hope and that what he gives to people matters.

Brent also accompanied me on one of my trips to Ground Zero in the months after 9/11. He spent a week with a youth group serving food to people who had been displaced and devastated by the tragedy. He called me late one night and said, *"I just want to tell you I love you and I'm so glad we have a family and a home."* And I'm thinking, *"What happened?"* He told me that he realized all of these people had parents and spouses and kids who were never coming home. It impacted him substantially and still does to this day.

These are the lessons that help us not only raise children, but raise hope inside them so that when they get older they can contribute to others.

FAITH, HOPE AND LOVE

I've watched hope go out of people when a crisis or tragedy hits. They just stop, because life as they know it is over. Well, it is, but refusing to give up hope allows a new life to spring forth. Like the seed that has to die unto itself before it can become a plant, a tragedy asks us to keep on hoping, while letting go of the life we once had.

As I said, in addition to psychology, I also have a background in theology because I wanted to fully understand life. I didn't believe psychology was enough. In the Bible, First Corinthians, chapter 13, there is the greatest definition of love I've ever seen. It says you may have complete power or knowledge or even sacrifice, but without love, your life is nothing. At the end, the passage says (13:13): "But now faith, hope and love remain—these three; and the greatest of these is love." You may solve many mysteries or move mountains, *but love is the purpose of life*.

Another Bible passage, Hebrews 11:1, says: "Now faith is the substance of things hoped for, the evidence of things not seen." Faith is the substance—the paint on the brush—of the things we hope for. But hope is the canvas it's painted on. And what we ultimately hope for is love: the unconditional acceptance of ourselves and others. In Greek, three types of love exist: Philia, the love of friendship and family; Eros, the love of sex and passion; and Agape, a God-like unconditional love or acceptance, and the deepest kind of love. All three types of love imbue meaning and purpose into our lives.

So love is the ultimate goal and it takes faith to live, but *hope* is the trinity manifested through time. It's mentioned in the middle, not as a bookend. Hope is in the middle of two very important things—it's the glue that holds together faith and love. If you lose hope, you skew the painting of your life and instead create pain, sadness or hatred. Our hope comes to life in the words we use, the choices we make and our relationships. *We're always painting pictures to reflect what we hope for. Our deepest inspiration is to do something with that substance of faith onto the canvas of hope, so we can paint a life of love.*

We simply need to make sure we have hope in something greater than ourselves. If we only hope in *ourselves*, we're going to be limited. Hoping for success or beauty will feel empty at the end of your life. So what if I made all of this money, or accumulated nice things? Life is meant to be enjoyed and spent in the moment! We must hope in something bigger than "I."

Hope is the adhesive that holds a life together. Hope is "The Gift."

Chapter 12
The Strength of Surrender

"Self-interest is but the survival of the animal in us.
Humanity only begins for man with self-surrender."
– Henri Frederic Amiel

Surrender is our greatest power. The concept of surrender is an odd one, because most people perceive it as a weakness. If you surrender to someone or something, the common thinking goes, you are inferior. As a result, most of us try to do the opposite. We try to control or dominate our circumstances and relationships.

In fact, surrender offers us the *greatest* influence in our lives. I define surrender as yielding to another person or thing. While surrender may look like weakness on the outside, it literally works as a magnet to pull positive energy and growth to you. This may come in the form of a new strength or skill, learned from submitting to a force you can't control. It may come in the shape of a new life opportunity, which never would have come your way had you not surrendered to a challenging situation. Or, it may be a person who you attract into your life because of your service and influence. Surrender can be the pathway to the love we seek, with both current and future partners.

I define healthy love as the positive possession of each other. When you're in love, you possess someone to the point that they need you and you them. However, there is a strong difference between what most people think of possession—which can have an almost demonic connotation—and positive possession. Positive possession is becoming part of someone by meeting *their* needs. It's almost reverse psychology. How many people dream that their current relationships were more loving or that the perfect love will come their way? Many are searching for the love of their life, that utopian state of perfection, and don't realize *they* hold the power to make it happen.

Meeting another person's need's can powerfully bring you the love you seek. It's a paradox. The great psychologist, Abraham Maslow, wrote about the hierarchy of needs. Everybody seeks to have their basic *needs* met. It's our desires that are more of an option (which is why many people get in unfulfilling relationships and just settle—their needs are met, but not necessarily their desires).

The paradox of surrender is that yielding to someone or something is an investment that comes back to you. I had to learn to surrender to Brandon's disability, and allow it to shape me in the way it did. Otherwise, I would have ended up an angry, indignant and hostile person. It didn't happen overnight, but I finally learned to surrender to it. And I ended up helping myself as much as, if not more than, I helped Brandon. In meeting his needs, my needs were also met in a deferred way and that's what allows me to help others.

SURRENDER IS POWER

The first skill that military recruits learn from their training is the power of submission. It's why there are drill sergeants in the first place: to break down the recruits, then build them back up in the confidence of having surrendered to authority. Men and women who aren't able to submit to authority in early training never make it to the next level of service. Successful military recruits know there is a purpose to this exercise and they have a destination in mind.

A similar dynamic applies in everyday life. For the vast majority of citizens, if a police officer flashes his lights and wants to pull you over, you stop. It's simply what you do. However, if you're a bank robber or a drug dealer, you won't surrender so easily. You have too much to lose. Surrender comes down to understanding your motive. If your motive is to be a good citizen, you're going to surrender to police. If your motive is to steal, cheat or avoid the consequences of your actions, you will challenge the police's authority.

Any relationship can be maximized by the act of surrender. However, I want to clarify the difference between power and authority. Authority is power under control. A person with healthy authority chooses to use their power correctly, rather than to dominate or abuse someone. Naturally, there are many people and situations in life that fall short of meeting this definition and, in those instances, it's always important to protect yourself.

However, in the majority of relationships and life challenges, your safety is not on the line. As I like to say, there are no dead bodies, so we need to rise to the occasion and discover what lesson this life experience is here to teach us. Often, we start by trying to "take charge." We say we're going to quit this terrible job or we're going to beat this illness or we're finished with a difficult relationship in our lives. Some situations are, indeed, fixable. However, others have a way of repeating themselves, which is usually a sign that we are responding in the wrong way and we have yet to learn the lesson at hand. Sometimes, the act of surrender—giving into the person or thing that is plaguing us—is what's needed for us to discover our power over it. We are only powerless if we give up.

Children, as much as they may fight it, have no choice but to surrender. They depend on their parents for love, sustenance and survival. As adults, there remains a similar power in surrendering to others. You're yielding out of a personal power, not weakness. If you're not threatened by the person or thing you're yielding to, you're an equal or even *superior* to that authority because you're not intimidated by it.

People often confuse power and weakness for this reason. They say, *"I'm not going to let this person have the upper hand."* And I say, "They just want to have their needs met, whether it's a boss, a spouse or a friend! They're going to meet your needs once you start meeting theirs."

SURRENDER IS LOVE

People say marriage is 50/50. It's not. Marriage is 100/100. It requires everything you've got to make it work: 100% of your body, your finances, your intellect and your love. The power of making sure you're not threatened by giving 100% comes from surrendering to your spouse.

In most traditional relationships, the man is going to be the dominant person because of higher testosterone levels. Testosterone is the hormone that drives dominance, aggression and libido. Of course, there are always exceptions, but even in gay or lesbian relationships, someone is always going to be the dominant one. The person who realizes they are less dominant in the relationship, and again this is in a normal relationship without abuse or pathology, can discover a power in surrendering to their partner.

In the Bible, the book of Ephesians (5:22) says, "Wives, submit to your husbands as to the Lord." The interpretation of this single line has been widely misunderstood and distorted through the years. Men tend to think, *"That's what I'm talking about!"* Women think, *"I'm not doing that!"* And we end up with a misconception of what it means, which takes the next five to six sentences to figure out (and which many people never get to!). Basically, these sentences go on to say that if a wife submits to her husband, he will come back, in time, and give her what she needs. Honor your husband and you lead the way to a better relationship. If anything, this passage basically says to stroke the male ego and you'll get what you want. A wife who submits will find her husband adores and loves her. What man doesn't want to be honored, and what woman doesn't want to be adored?

If the less dominant person surrenders to the more dominant, the more dominant person will actually come back and surrender to that person. I've seen it over and over again. I'll be coaching a woman who's having trouble in her marriage and say, *"The way to get to your husband to respond to you is by submitting to him."* And in most cases, she'll respond, *"You don't understand, he's trying to control me! He ignores me!"* And I'll say, *"If you understand submitting in its purest form, which is bowing to that power and person—not trying to control him—you will draw that person back to you.*"

I say, "*Just try it.*" And the woman does it, then comes back next week and says, "*That's amazing, it worked!*" Eventually, the woman feels comforted, protected and cared for by her husband. She realizes she is getting her needs met, by submitting. It's not weak; it's actually for the benefit of her relationship and herself.

Similarly, I will tell men, "*Stop trying to control or dominate your wife. Just love her, unconditionally.*" When she asks you if she looks fat, she's not looking for your opinion. She's looking for your love and acceptance. In effect, her question is, "*Do you love me even though I feel fat*"? For the man, the right answer is one of reassurance, rather than having his say. It goes against logic and truth sometimes. Even if she does look a little pudgy, surrendering is more important. You may have to surrender to the ideal of what you would like her to look like, but at the end of the day, it's more important to love her than to focus only on the physical attribute of appearance. You'll create that inspiration in her to be all that she can be by loving her and accepting her through your behavioral example.

The power in surrendering is understanding that each person needs to step out of their ego long enough to serve the relationship, rather than trying to win their point. It doesn't matter if you're right (as long as it's legal and ethical). It's really about the long haul, the relationship. Surrender teaches you the ability to compromise and as long as you're getting some of your needs met, you're ahead of the game. No one gets their needs met *all* of the time and if you do, you're spoiled like a child.

The reason people abuse others in marriage, emotionally or physically, is because they don't know how to surrender. In a primitive way, they're trying to dominate the other person by abusing them. The first key to not abusing someone is to surrender to them. Surrendering allows the *relationship* to become the dominant force, instead of one person being the dominant force, and relationship equilibrates.

When we surrender and the other person surrenders, the unit becomes the strongest entity—not either individual. That's why marriage is 100/100, not 50/50. If you're giving 50/50, you're holding something back and the relationship isn't going to work. The scariest part of marriage is being able to reveal yourself mentally, emotionally, spiritually and physically, without worrying that the other person is going to reject or control you.

It takes a secure person to be able to do it. There's no way an insecure person is going to submit, because they're afraid of what will happen. They're sure they'll be taken advantage of or forgotten. That's why they keep "score" or refuse to ever be in the weaker position. However, if you feel strong in yourself, you're going to reap the benefits of surrender without keeping score.

When you surrender, you're not giving up, but rather giving in to the greater result.

SURRENDER IS CONNECTION

Parenting works in a similar way. Instead of trying to dominate a child, you have to get into a child's space and try to learn from him or her, in addition to creating boundaries and discipline, which will draw the child to you. Parenting is especially trying in adolescence. You can no longer simply make decisions for your children. You have to finesse the situation and figure out what makes them tick to make the relationship work for both of you. You have to temper your dominance if you want to continue nourishing a healthy, happy relationship into adulthood.

I discovered this in my life because I was dating and married to my wife for 27 years. That's nearly all of my adult life. Now that I'm single again, I've learned even more that if you surrender to another person early on, you'll win. This is very different from the usual approach and information available about dating. Rather than focusing on my own wants and needs, I choose to listen more than I speak, because I know that's the key. I'm going to discover the information that's there and allow the other person to reveal herself, and use that information to create the relationship. It's a whole learning process of trying to figure out why people respond the way they do and what they're all about.

Everyone puts their best foot forward in the beginning of dating, but that's not really who that person is. By focusing on the other person from the start, instead of on myself, I know that person's true self is going to be revealed. Both the good and the bad qualities of that person are allowed to come through. It allows the relationship to proceed from a foundation of truth from as early as possible, so we can discover if we're genuinely compatible and interested in each other.

SURRENDER TO YOURSELF

When I did premarital counseling, I saw a couple in their 20s who said they got along great and never fought. I told them to put together a list of expectations for each other and bring it with them next time, when we would review it together. The night before our next session, they had a huge fight after going through their lists! At our session the next day, they realized they weren't really being honest with each other and sharing their deepest needs up to this point. After talking it through, they ended up surrendering to each other and realized that a fight wasn't going to kill them. Rather, it could make them both more real with each other.

Someone is lying if you never disagree. Couples need to disagree to discover each other. What one partner wants and needs may offend or freak out the other, but it's not going to break you. A *good fight* allows you to surrender to each other in an authentic way and discover the treasure of your relationship. Ultimately, a relationship isn't finding someone you can live with, but finding someone *you can't live without*. You can learn to live with anyone.

It's the same with any relationship. If you only share what you think a person wants to hear, rather than what you really have to say, you'll never be truly known by that person (or anyone if this is how you operate in most of your relationships). If I have a force-field activated around me, which is literally the human ego, to protect me from people who are going to hurt me or control me, I'm not going to communicate fully. Becoming open and letting that guard down is a risk and it feels dangerous. But it's what's required to have a real relationship. Communication is the oil that keeps relationships lubricated and running smoothly. You have to be vulnerable and penetrable with another person to be real with them.

Understanding that the true value in any relationship—whether romantic, parental or professional—comes from *surrendering,* which is the hidden power that most people never see. "The Gift" of surrender is a doorway to our best and most satisfying relationships, with others and also with ourselves.

Chapter 13
Death Is A Beginning

"Death is not the greatest loss in life. The greatest loss is what dies inside of us while we live."
– Norman Cousins

All of us are born with an expiration date. Life has a 100% mortality rate. No one is going to survive life.

However, I don't mean this in a morbid way. The most important lesson we can learn about death is that it's *not* morbid. Death is as natural as birth. We tend to look at death as morbid because we see it as a loss. Of course, death is painful and sad; no one wants to lose a friend or loved one. However, life itself is a loss in training. As you've learned throughout this book, the power is in the perception. Life and death are more similar than we imagine, and death can inform life if we approach it in the right way.

In generations past, we were more natural about death. I vividly remember my grandparents talking about death. It was a very normal part of life and the life cycle. Each year, my grandparents and others in their life would hold a sort of "Memorial Day" for loved ones who had passed away. They celebrated, remembering that person's life and what they meant to them.

Today, we've put death away. We've brushed it under the rug and gone into a mass denial, which bubbles to the surface in other ways, like substance abuse, damaged relationships and depression. We deny death and, in doing so, we deny ourselves the gifts of death. We also deprive ourselves of the proper grieving process after death.

We can learn from cultures that celebrate death and see it as a doorway to another dimension. In these cultures, death is merely a pit stop along an eternal journey, not *The End!* The Mexican culture celebrates "Day of the Dead" to commemorate loved ones who are no longer with them. They read poems, laugh, create mementos and celebrate death as a continuation of life. The Greek culture throws parties after a loved one's funeral. In Japan, a Buddhist festival called Obon honors the spirits of those who have departed, with dance and visits to their graves.

Ultimately, death simply means that life in *this space* ends; however, I believe there is an eternal value in all of us that lives on. Death is very natural. What matters is how we handle it.

THE IMMORTAL TOUCH

Life's reach extends far beyond the grave. When we touch people's lives around us and they touch ours, that touch is eternal because it continues throughout life and beyond. When we die, it doesn't mean we're finished influencing the lives of those we knew. The English word "memory" roughly means "souvenir" in French. A memory is a souvenir we've gotten in life. Just as when we go on a trip and one souvenir allows us to recall an entire vacation, so does life become the accumulation of many souvenirs in our mind. When someone dies, we have many souvenirs of them and simply need to visit these memories to remember who they were.

We all have an everlasting and immortal touch on the lives of those around us. For this reason, there is no such thing as *not* having an influence on people—you either have a good influence or a bad influence. You're either a positive or a negative force, or a healthy or unhealthy one. There is a great quote from televangelist Mike Murdock that says: *"You will only be remembered for two things: the problems you solve or the ones you create."*

We're either inspiring or expiring the people around us. In the daily scheme of things, we are, by the way we live, either an inspiration to people or an expiration to them. Figuratively speaking, we either give life or we give death. Think about what happens to people in the presence of an inspiring *leader*. They become energized, pumped and ready to take on the world. People under the *dictatorship* of a negative person become pessimistic and unmotivated. Morale plummets and hope fades. When we live positively, we inspire others to positive living. By living negatively, we put expiration dates on our own lives and on those who we influence. This influence continues for all of eternity since, like souvenirs on a shelf, we are forever captured in the memory of each person's mind.

There is life after death; it's simply another dimension that continues to influence people after we've gone. Just as the gift of *time* provides a future effect on people, when we act we're investing in that moment in time, but also in the future. We're eternal in ways we never imagined, and grasping death is the way to maximize the immortal touch we leave on others.

I still remember things my dad said to me years ago. I can still hear him saying them, and I say them now. His inspiration and life still lives through me.

Life is the journey between birth and death and the influence of our life goes on forever. It's eternal.

DEATH PERCEPTION

When we inspire someone, it empowers us in the process, too. We're called upon to recognize death as natural, which enables us to be our best selves. We flip that coin and accept death, rather than fighting it or fearing it. Death is a normal part of life. It's going to happen whether we like it or not. Grasping this fact helps us get the most out of each and every day. If we live our life knowing that it's linear—it begins and ends—we'll be able to maximize the space between birth and death.

We tend to think of death as an end, rather than a beginning. We focus on the loss, instead of on the lessons of death. However, I think the philosophy of living comes out of a person's perception of dying. *When you appreciate dying, you learn to live in its presence and celebrate the moments of living while slowly moving with gravity toward death.*

I learned this with my son, Brandon. Year after year of being told he was going to die and wondering if every day would be my last with him, I came to grips with his mortality and, in the process, the fact of my mortality. Instead of waiting for him to die, I finally said, "*Why not experience living with him today?*"

I've seen people for whom death was a gift, because the loss of that loved one inspired them to start living their life to the fullest. Death propelled them forward into life, instead of trapping them in memories of the past. It's the difference between *surviving* your life versus *living* your life. We only get one shot! Life and time are linear. Every moment that ticks by is another moment gone. We can either live life to the fullest, or watch it pass us by. Life doesn't stop for anyone; you've got to "jump on" and learn to ride the wave.

I think what's powerful about this death perception is that it aligns us with an essential truth: our whole life is about learning. Children learn from the moment they're born. Their nervous systems are impregnable, logging information and discovering new things about the world and themselves as they grow into themselves. The fact that many of us miss as adults is that we're designed to do this for the rest of our lives.

I can't tell you how many people stop learning or observing or growing because they think they have it all figured out. People who are depressed often get to this point. They stop living or they actually want to end their life because they *can't* live it anymore. They can't flip that coin. They're stuck. As I mentioned earlier, the best medicine for a depressed person is to get out of themselves by serving another. They need to see that life is still there to reveal itself and create meaning and opportunity for them, but it usually requires getting out of one's mind.

At the other end of the spectrum are powerful people with enormous egos who don't appreciate what they have. They've lost their grasp on reality because they overvalue their life, without realizing their connection to others. I see this in many successful athletes and businessmen. They've achieved staggering levels of success, but their ego has grown right along with it. They have the whole world in their hands, but they'll complain about the smallest challenge or pettiest grievance. They're living a dream life compared to most people and they don't even understand the meaning of it all. When I hear an athlete, for instance, complain about his job, I tell him, *"You play a game for a living*! I think it's going to be ok! You're going to make it."

I like growing older because I've learned to work smarter, not harder. I appreciate my successes *and* my challenges more now. I know the moment I stop learning is the moment I choose to die, because life is a constant learning experience. There are two great equalizers in life: we're all born and we all die. No one was hatched or beamed down! *And no one is going to outrun death.* You can facelift and dye your hair, but you're not going to avoid death. It's inevitable. We must come to grips with this eventually. No matter what you do, how you look or who you are, you're still a person who's going to live and die. We need to live life to such a full state that we don't avoid death, but embrace it. *We allow it to inspire us to the point that we live life to the fullest.*

Birth and death: we all do it the same way and life is what happens in between.

LIFE IS A ONE-WAY JOURNEY

I define time as the space between past eternity and future eternity. We all share time—a mental, emotional, spiritual and physical navigational dimension. We need to respect that fact. No one is better than anyone else and no one deserves more out of life than any other person. There wouldn't be crime if we had true equality and sharing. The irony is that there is enough time for everybody; we just have to figure out how to portion it.

I always tell people there is enough money out there, but you have to figure out how to get it into your bank account. The same applies to people and relationships. There's a whole world of people out there and you can choose whom you spend your time with. Wasting time in bad relationships or one-sided friendships is a choice, not an inevitability. *It's never too late—or too early—to change your life.*

For teens and kids especially, one person or group can change the whole trajectory of a person's life. One wrong choice takes you down a path that may be quite different than the potential inside of you. When you're young, it's easy to feel immortal, in the sense that you'll be here on earth forever. You don't grasp the weight of your decisions or how you may be diverting your true purpose.

Prisons are full of people with destiny locked up inside them. They made one or more wrong decisions about what life had to offer them, by stealing or killing or manipulating the system. They didn't think there was enough life for them and, paradoxically, they limit what their life could have been. I spent time counseling people on death row, and more than anything, they talked about their regrets of not being able to live the potential that's locked up inside of them, never to come to life.

Years ago, when I was very young and just starting out in my training, I was introduced to a woman named Lorane who was dying of cancer. I met her at the hospital, at the end of stage IV cancer. All medical interventions had been performed and she was basically waiting to die.

I would see Lorane a couple of times a week. I would visit and just talk to her, trying to cheer her up and flip that coin, helping her see the goodness of her family and her life. As the days went on, she was getting worse and one night when I had to go to dinner, she asked me to stay and continue telling her stories. Every time I would try to leave, she kept asking me to stay just a little while longer. Because of my dinner obligation, I finally told her I had to go. I left, and went to dinner late.

I got a call about an hour later that Lorane had died after I left. She had known she was going to die, but couldn't verbalize it to me at the hospital. In my youth and inexperience, I didn't see that and interpret it correctly. I felt terrible and as though I had let her down for quite some time. But eventually, I came to grips with the fact of mortality and that I had done all I could. Most of all, I realized she had wanted to share her life as much as she could, right up until the very end.

BORN TO LIVE

We're all born with sheets of music in us. I don't want to go to the grave with any music left in me. I'm going to karaoke my way all the way to the grave! That's why I write and talk to people, because it makes a difference in someone's life—even if it's just one person, it's worth it. I've touched someone's life in a positive way.

Imagine the one person who made the biggest impact on Martin Luther King, Jr. or Mother Teresa. Can you imagine going back to that person and saying it was no big deal? Without that person, we never would have had Martin Luther King, Jr., or Mother Teresa, and the course of history would have been changed forever. We never know the impact we are having on another person's life and what the fruits of that immortal touch may bear someday.

That's the power of life: understanding that we're all going to die and deciding what we want to leave behind. Are you going to leave behind music unsung, or are you going to sing it loud and proud to everyone? We all have that power and only *we* can do it for ourselves. Imagination and creativity are born and still live inside all of us. The question is: Are we using it? And how?

Countless people right now are waiting to live their life after they meet the right person, after they lose weight, after they get rich, after retirement. However, many studies find that physical and mental health begins to decline soon after retirement. That's because many people lose their sense of purpose. I don't want to live my life to be retired! I want to be "retired" today, even if I have to go to work. Turn your vocation into a vacation! Turn your life into *right now* by refusing to live for the future. The moment is all we've got.

Life is what we're after. You can't have life without a birth and you can't appreciate life without a healthy perspective of death. That's the importance of being able to embrace death, and understand it.

Death is the ultimate "Gift." Live your life. Don't just survive it. *Unwrap it today and celebrate your gift.* Then give to others to do the same thing!

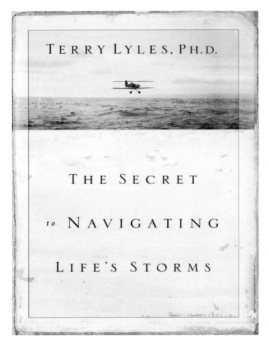

TERRY LYLES, PH.D.

THE SECRET

to NAVIGATING

LIFE'S STORMS

This book assists parents, families, executives and elite performers in the quest for living life to the fullest each day, without losing personal health, happiness and daily productivity. *The Secret to Navigating Life's Storms* is a collection of inspiring and uplifting stories form years of work with professional athletes, corporate executive, military Special Forces and the professionals and volunteers at Ground Zero. Dr. Lyles also share his own personal stories of raising two children, one who is quadriplegic and wheelchair bound for twenty years and shares how he empowered and motivated himself and those around him to remain optimistic about what is truly possible through the correct utilization of daily stress. Dr. Lyles' honest and humorous approach is both touching and engaging, providing us an excellent framework for handling stress well in any situation.

In this ground-breaking new work, America's Stress Doctor, Terry Lyles, Ph.D. shows you how to transform stress into a positive source of vital energy for living younger longer. Good Stress presents us with the ultimate paradoxical challenge: seeing life's stressful challenges as positive and potentially life-enhancing. Ignoring stress or interpreting it as negative denies us important opportunities for growth and achievement that stress provides. In *Good Stress*, Dr. Lyles provides you with powerful insights and simple exercises that will enable you to reach higher levels of performance and satisfaction in every area of life.

Through his work with victims, volunteers and relief workers at many of the world's natural disaster sites (9/11, Hurricane Katrina and the Asian tsunami) as well as with high-performance elite athletes and military personnel, Dr. Lyles has helped thousands of people to overcome apparently insurmountable odds and use stress to propel them to higher levels of success and wellness. Now, through training and application, you too can enjoy the benefits of Good Stress and begin living younger longer.

162

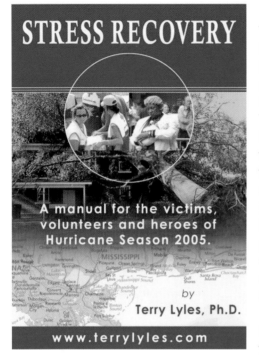

STRESS RECOVERY

A manual for the victims, volunteers and heroes of Hurricane Season 2005.

by
Terry Lyles, Ph.D.

www.terrylyles.com

The Stress Recovery Manual was a blessing in the wake of a record-setting 2005 hurricane season. Dr. Terry Lyles, America's Stress Doctor, donated thousands of hours to the volunteers, victims and heroes of **Hurricanes Katrina, Rita** and **Wilma** – people who were subjected to enormous amounts of hardship and challenges.

Now you can benefit from his time-tested and scientifically-measured approach to stress utilization.

"This manual is applicable to anyone wanting to improve their relationship to stress," says Dr. Lyles, who for the past 10 years has trained hundreds of individuals, including fire rescue workers in and around **Ground Zero**, international forensic medical teams in **tsunami-torn Asia**, and those affected by the **hurricanes**. Dr. Lyles has also trained top executives, managers and employees in Fortune 500 companies and the U.S. Government as well as professional athletes.